Early Acclaim for BlindSpots™

With *BlindSpots* Lynn Collins and Barbara McDuffie do a great job of pointing out how to identify and counteract those subtle aspects of our lives that prevent us from reaching our true potential. We'd all be better off with this book on our shelves.

> Robert B. Cialdini, PhD, author of *Influence: Science and Practice* and *Influence: The Psychology of Persuasion.*

For most of us, it takes nearly a lifetime to escape the patterns of behavior that limit our possibilities. This book provides a pathway to an unstuck future for each of us.

> John Lathrop, Director, Executive Learning, Daniels School of Business, University of Denver.

A wise, well thought out book written with compassion and humor which will inspire anyone who wants to unmask their BlindSpots on any level. You'll read it more than once.

> Peter McWilliams, best selling author of the *Life 101* Series.

An easy to read masterpiece, blending humor, truth and practical coaching. This book does the impossible by making BlindSpots irresistible and amusing.

Jane Bluestein, PhD, author of *Daily Riches* and *Creating Emotionally Safe Schools.*

Collins and McDuffie scored so many direct hits that I thought they must have written the book specifically for me! Readers will no doubt recognize their own blind spots in this straightforward, often entertaining guide for making intelligent life choices. Profound common sense strategies for change were never more accessible. Keep a fresh highlighter at the ready. You'll be applying it often to the pages of BlindSpots.

Joseph P. Reel, PhD, Creator of Human Development Training Programs and *Bardo Therapy* Training Tapes.

This book unravels our perceptual layers one by one, like pulling glue apart in a gentle, clear and step by step way to actually change how and what we see.

Valerie Berg, Certified Advanced Rolfer®, Rolf Institute Faculty.

BlindSpots

Your Psychological SpeedBumps

**Dr. Lynn Collins &
Barbara McDuffie**

To order additional copies of this book, contact:
Xlibris Corporation
1-888-795-4274
www.Xlibris.com
Orders@Xlibris.com
20076

CONTENTS

SECTION ONE: MEET THE BLINDSPOTS

SECTION TWO: BLINDSPOT STRATEGY

SECTION THREE: I THINK I'VE SPOTTED ONE

SECTION FOUR: THE ROAD NOT TAKEN

DEAR READER:

If you have picked up this book, we assume you have some curiosity about who we are and we assume you want to know about BlindSpots. We would like to tell you we are people who have successfully and completely eradicated all our BlindSpots and have been inoculated against developing any in the future.

Unfortunately, we can't say that. We don't believe anyone can. What we can say is we are committed and willing to see our own BlindSpots and do whatever it takes to find them amusing enough to continue looking. We are dedicated to helping anyone who is on a similar path.

We invite you to look for your BlindSpots as we coach you through our book. (If you don't want to find your BlindSpots, put this book down immediately!)

Since you're still reading, we invite you to stay curious as you explore, discover, and learn. We promise you things will never be quite the same again.

Your coaches,

Lynn Collins and Barabara McDuffie
The SpotDoctors™

INTRODUCTION TO
BLINDSPOTS

We believe you have BlindSpots to uncover – and this book removes the blindfold again and again.

In our work coaching, teaching, and counseling, we have discovered and identified automatic patterns of thought and behavior which keep you from getting what you want. We noticed people had these patterns – patterns that were clear to us and surprisingly invisible to them. We were amazed how often this phenomenon occurred in everyone with whom we worked. Then we noticed it showed up equally as often with friends, family, total strangers, and alas, even ourselves. We called them "BlindSpots" and they are apparently everywhere.

FORWARD

This book was written to assist anyone who might have a BlindSpot. *This book was written for everyone.*

This book was written to help. *It is not a substitute for therapy. It might make you consider therapy. It might be a starting point for therapy. It might explain, encourage, or support some therapy. It could make you yearn for therapy for people you know. Just remember, even though it can be therapeutic, this book is not therapy.*

By reading **"BlindSpots,"** *we hope you're lead to clarity and awareness that can change some of your patterns successfully and easily, thereby changing your life in the direction you'd like it to go.*

This book was written to amuse and enlighten. *We don't believe change or learning happens easily without some degree of perspective and amusement. We offer some of both.*

We consider BlindSpots a serious topic – much too serious to be taken too seriously. We have found that things taken too seriously are often frightening, intimidating, boring, and/or difficult.

After working with thousands of people, we find that something that is too hard, frightening, intimidating, or difficult will guarantee most people remain stuck in their old, easy, safe, and familiar patterns. And certainly, if something is boring, most people will easily give it up.

When people are smiling and laughing, they are processing information in a very productive way. You will have to "get it" to be amused. And when you "get it" and are amused, you're more likely to do something about it. It's also difficult to be frightened when you're amused. We're taking a light touch with BlindSpots, because we believe it makes the frightening more exciting and the difficult easier.

This book was written about *real* people. *We anticipate you'll read some of our stories and exclaim, "This couldn't possibly be true." But it is.*

We've changed every name to protect the innocent and the guilty – and to keep us from being sued. We took poetic license in some cases to compress several examples into a more coherent and amusing retelling. We've told you what we heard people say. We've told you what they said they were thinking. And in some cases, we did a little creative mind reading and imagined what they must have been thinking in order to act as they did.

We wish to thank all the people who have demonstrated BlindSpots to us over the years. They dutifully contributed their patterns and foibles again and again. Without their stories, BlindSpots might not amuse you at all.

ACKNOWLEDGMENTS

We are deeply grateful to so many people for their contribution to this book. Obviously, all the people who have allowed us to observe their patterns have made this book possible. The people who taught us, both in and out of school, are reflected on every page. The people we've coached have always taught us as much as we might have taught them. Those lessons are a big part of *BlindSpots*.

Special thanks to the artist Eric Velhagen who understood how the BlindSpots had to look and drew the originals for us. We are very grateful to our two art directors, Sandy Hill and Lisa Abreo, for their contribution to the symbolic renderings within these pages. Nothing was included unless we thought it clear, to the point, and amusing.

This book wouldn't exist if it weren't for our editor and good friend, Gail Harvey. She has invested so many hours and so much faith in *BlindSpots*. She has pushed us to express our thoughts with clarity. She has compromised when the *correct* way to say something sounded more stiff and stilted than we could stand. We promised to tell you that anything which doesn't read in an impeccable way probably made her teeth itch and she's not responsible it's still said that way – we are.

We thank our families for the many different ways throughout our lifetime that they have contributed to the concepts found in *BlindSpots*.

We have had many authors, business people, and therapists encourage our work and keep us on track. We are particularly grateful for the help and guidance offered by Peter McWilliams and saddened by his untimely death.

We are grateful to BlindSpots everywhere for all the ways they contribute to psychological, emotional, and spiritual growth in humans. And we're full of admiration for anyone who decides to see a BlindSpot and take him to doggie school.

BlindSpots – Section ONE

Meet the BlindSpots – Spot, Spot, and Spot.

Here is your opportunity to get acquainted with the BlindSpots. What do they look like? Where do they show up? What are they up to?
This is the first step in getting comfortable with spotting Spot.
The BlindSpots can be anywhere – behind the curtain, under the rug, inside a container, or right under your nose.

CHAPTER ONE

Is This Just a Bunch of BS?

Absolutely! This entire book is about BS, the abbreviation for BlindSpots.

The good news is that everyone has BS. The bad news is that you can usually see everyone else's BS much more easily than you can see your own. You're more perceptive and resourceful regarding everyone else's BlindSpots. You usually think you know what the other person should do, and you often tell them. If you don't tell the individual, you tell someone else. You have lots to say about other people's BS. This propensity to notice only other people's BlindSpots could be a BlindSpot of your own.

What exactly are BlindSpots? BlindSpots are invisible, automatic patterns of behavior, thoughts, or feelings that can sabotage your success and happiness. They are, very simply, things you cannot see which are in your way – SpeedBumps™ in your road. BlindSpots are hidden. They exist behind the curtain, under the rug, and in the closet – until you're ready to see them.

The stories you're about to read are all true. Only the names have been changed to protect the BlindSpotted.

Nick's story:

> One day ten-year old Nick stormed into his house, rubbing a nasty cut on his forehead. "Dad," he whined, "you have to cut that tree limb that hangs over the driveway. I keep hitting my head on it every time I walk by!" Nick's dad raised his eyebrows in surprise and responded, "You know, son, I only hit my head on it once."

Nick was missing some key pieces. But those pieces were very visible to his dad. Nick's dad had no BlindSpot regarding the limb. He simply avoided it after the first time he bumped into it. But Nick, even though he knew the limb was there and had whacked his head on it every time he walked by, didn't change his strategy. Amazingly, Nick continued to whack his head on the same limb. Predictably (to the BlindSpot-savvy), Nick continued to get the same result . . . every time! This is a BlindSpot.

Whatever Nick kept saying to himself to keep alternatives invisible is probably another BlindSpot. We're often – unconsciously and invisibly – taking ourselves deeper into an automatic behavior without even realizing it.

Before you get too smug about Nick, notice you may have a few symbolic tree limbs that you continue to bump. And like Nick, you keep crashing into them, blaming the limb or blaming someone else for not getting the limb out of your way. If you have any awareness of a pattern like this, you are uncovering a BlindSpot right now! If you think you have no patterns like this, you are uncovering a BlindSpot right now! (You're starting to see how it works, aren't you?)

BlindSpots can show up virtually any time, but they persistently follow disappointment, conflict, stress, anger, resistance, or change. When BlindSpots are activated you will do things, say things, think things, and feel things that undermine the situation and magnetically take you in the direction you least want to go. You repeat behaviors just as Nick did when he continued to whack his head with the tree limb. And, just like Nick, until you can see the BlindSpot, you're doomed to keep whacking.

Sometimes the BlindSpot remains invisible just because you have been doing the same things the same way for so long.

Congress' story:

> Every day, for over 100 years, two buckets of ice were delivered to the offices of each member of the U. S. House of Representatives. This practice began long before modern refrigeration. However, it continued 60 years after all the Representatives had personal refrigerators with icemakers in their offices.

That's right. Two buckets of ice were delivered to people with icemakers for 60 years. And that's not all. Where do you think the buckets of ice were placed when they were delivered? The two buckets of ice were always placed on the floor directly beside the refrigerator with the icemaker – a cost to the taxpayer of $500,000 per year. That's a $30 million dollar BlindSpot.

This was a Congressional BlindSpot, of which there are many. It stands out, like most BlindSpots, because it is so simple and obvious . . . once spotted. It was obvious, apparently, to all but those closest to the ice. No one noticed or stopped this unnecessary and wasteful practice until 1997. The deliveries of ice were so automatic, the absurdity of their continuation was invisible to everyone until some alert BlindSpotter finally took note.

Like that BlindSpotter, you can decide to remove your blindfold any time. If you continue to leave it on and act as if there is nothing in your life that needs to be noticed or changed, you will pay a high price for your complacency. BlindSpots can sabotage relationships, time, money, and both professional and personal success and happiness. Listen to the SpotDoctors and you will begin to notice the SpeedBumps that slow you down. You will begin to notice the limbs repeatedly whacking your head. You will begin to notice the unnecessary buckets of ice being delivered to your refrigerator.

Undetected BlindSpots can make life much more difficult for you, just as it did for 88-year old Myrtle.

Myrtle's story:

Each morning Myrtle followed the same routine. She awakened at 5:30 a.m., got dressed, made her bed, said her prayers, and started the coffee. Myrtle had been practicing the same pattern day after day, year after year, decade after decade. You get the point. This is a long-term automatic pattern. Up to this point it was an automatic pattern with no BlindSpot in sight, until . . .

One morning Myrtle awakened, looked at the clock, and was shocked to see that she'd slept until 6:00 a.m., something she never did. She jumped up and quickly engaged her automatic pattern – she got dressed, made the bed, and said her prayers. When she reached the point in her pattern where she made coffee, she looked at the clock in the kitchen. It read 12:45 a.m. – 45 minutes past midnight. The middle of the night.

She checked her bedside clock and it read 12:45 a.m. She realized she'd mixed up the hands of the clock. When she'd thought it was 6:00 a.m., it had actually been 12:30 a.m. She was up and dressed with her pattern fully engaged in the dark of night.

This is a book about BlindSpots, so you're probably way ahead of us. The sensible thing for Myrtle to do would have been to go back to bed and get her remaining five hours of rest. But a BlindSpot was afoot.

Myrtle stayed up the rest of the night and when her son asked her why she didn't just go back to bed, she replied in a matter-of-fact way, "I already made my bed."

Once Myrtle engaged her get-up-in-the-morning automatic pattern, there was no turning back. She seemed to be saying to herself, "Once the bed is made, I'm up, no matter what time of day."

Her son was flabbergasted that she was so rigid and inflexible. He couldn't understand how his mother, who was having real trouble keeping her sleepy little eyes open, could have sat up all night long just because her bed was already made.

This pattern may sound silly, or inconsequential, or obvious to you. Most BlindSpots, when revealed, appear silly, or bizarre, or obvious – once you really see them for what they are. While blindfolded, however, they seem quite sensible. You don't give them a second thought. Actually you don't give them a first thought . . . and that allows them to stay invisible.

Of course, like Myrtle, or Nick, or the individuals in Congress, you had some very good reasons for your BlindSpot patterns when you put them in place. We refer to the good reasons for starting or maintaining any pattern – future BlindSpot or not – as your positive Intentions. These are the goals and intentions – conscious or unconscious – which prompt your initial choices.

CHAPTER TWO

The Road to Your BlindSpots is Paved with Good Intentions

Intentions stand behind every choice you make, which makes spotting your BlindSpots tricky, difficult, but interesting. If you believe you are operating out of positive Intentions, then it seems logical that the automatic patterns that follow must also be positive, purposeful, logical, and "right." And sometimes they are. And sometimes they're not. Sometimes, even with the very best of Intentions in place, your automatics do you in.

Bonnie and Chester's story:

Chester, Bonnie's husband, was trying hard to get their new house fixed up. They desperately needed blinds in several rooms and he had promised Bonnie he would complete the project over the weekend. They went to House Depot together to pick up materials. All the way there, Chester kept telling her how important it was to get the right blinds, the correct attachments, and all the other gear, or she wasn't going to be happy with the job. He kept saying, "I just want to get it right, get it done, and make you happy."

They parked at House Depot and Bonnie went to the magazine section to look at room designs while Chester hustled to the blind aisle, focused and intent. She called after him to remember something and he didn't even hear her. Clearly he was concentrating very hard on "getting it right, getting it done, and getting her happy."

Bonnie was content to flip through the magazines, but noticed it was taking Chester a very long time to get back to her. She went looking in the blind aisle (at the time she had no idea how prophetic the aisle name was) – no Chester. Bonnie looked at the register – no Chester. She decided to check the parking lot and not only was there no Chester, there was no car either. He was gone – or kidnapped. Either way, Bonnie had a problem. She was alone at House Depot with no money, no purse, no change, no identification, and no way home – a full 15 miles away.

She went to a pay phone and placed a collect call to the house. Imagine how surprised she was when Chester answered the phone. As calmly as she could she said, "Chester, this is Bonnie, will you please come pick me up?" Chester replied, "I'm busy with the blinds. Where are you?" Through clenched teeth, Bonnie said, "I'm at House Depot."

"What are you doing there?" the intent blinds-installer asked.

"YOU LEFT ME HERE, YOU IDIOT!"

There was dead silence on the other end of the phone. "Well?" Bonnie said. "Oh dear,"

Chester murmured pathetically. "I'll be right there."

When he picked Bonnie up, apologizing profusely, she asked him how he could leave her and not even notice. Chester pleaded, "I was just so focused on the blinds. I knew how much you wanted them up. I just kept thinking how happy you'd be when the job was done. All the way home I was saying to myself how happy you were going to be. That's all I wanted was for you to be happy."

"Well, I'm not," Bonnie said.

"I completely understand," said Chester. "You know my intentions were really good." "Yes, dear," Bonnie responded, beginning to feel just a little sympathetic. "Good intentions, bad planning. I should have known when you went to the blind aisle by yourself, there would be trouble."

Chester was so focused on his Intention – his assignment to himself – that he completely lost sight of all the other considerations and ended up producing exactly the opposite result of what he wanted. He wanted to make his wife happy and that Intention focused exclusively on getting the blinds done. Because he allowed himself to go on AutoPilot™, he abandoned her at House Depot and, even when he heard her voice on the phone placing the collect call, didn't realize what he'd done. He was, after all, doing what his program told him to do – putting up the blinds.

Just like Chester, in an attempt to reach your goals, you generate behaviors to meet the needs of your Intentions. Many automatic patterns are just waiting to be tapped with an Intention. Your Intentions are as likely to be unconscious as they are to be conscious, but both drive your behavioral choices. Chester's Intentions were very conscious before he went unconscious. He had a wonderful Intention to make his wife happy, but it produced such a focused automatic set of behaviors that he was able to completely forget she was with him. The subsequent behavior made his wife very unhappy.

The quality of your Intention doesn't guarantee your automatic behaviors or any behaviors will produce successful results. As long as your Intentions are connected to a BlindSpot, you'll fail to see all your options. Correcting this kind of BlindSpot requires some honesty and introspection to determine where your Intentions go off track.

CHAPTER THREE

Are You as Honest as Alex?

Alex's story:

> Five-year old Alex wanted his busy mother
> to play his favorite board game with him. His
> mother suggested he set up the game beside her
> as she worked and play by himself – for both of
> them. Alex became tearful and replied, "I can't."
> When his mother asked why, he answered, "I
> can't play with me because I lie and I cheat."

Obviously, Alex is a BlindSpotter prodigy. Even though he was only five, he knew his own automatic pattern and saw how it made playing games with himself unappealing. Alex's insight into his own BlindSpot and recognition of the cost of his behavior represents a very high BlindSpotting Quotient. (You have IQ: Intelligence Quotient. You have EQ: Emotional Intelligence Quotient. Now you have BSQ™: BlindSpotting Quotient.)

The kind of introspection and honesty exhibited by Alex is rare, especially coming from a five-year old boy who "lies and cheats." We suspect that each of us may have an innate BlindSpotting ability, but we appear to lose it rather early in life. The advantage of having a high BSQ – or relearning it – is that it will propel you to search for new, more productive ChoicePoints™. You'll find places throughout your automatic patterns where alternative choices are available which might produce different or better results. There are still multiple dots for Alex to connect, but he's off to a productive start.

One ChoicePoint is to teach yourself to live happily with the pattern once it's visible and your choice is no longer hidden. If, like Alex, you discover where your actions are self-sabotaging, you are well on your way to unmasking BlindSpots, finding new ChoicePoints, and creating new, more successful patterns.

Your BSQ reflects how willing you are to spot your BlindSpots. No matter how high you think your BSQ is, it may still be uncomfortable to unmask BlindSpots. Predictably, people are afraid of what they don't know or what they may find. Whether you become an active BlindSpotter may hinge on whether you are one of those people who is willing to venture into your DiscomfortZone.

CHAPTER FOUR

Explaining the Dreaded DiscomfortZone™

We once heard that the only person who really loves change is a wet baby. We've met many people who claim to love change, and some of them really appear to cultivate change. But the one thing we notice, even about the most fearless change–seeker, is that they really only love it when it's the change they desire. The change-lovers don't seem so thrilled when having to address a change they didn't invite, weren't expecting, and don't like.

So we'd just like to go on record and declare that everyone has a DiscomfortZone. Some people like the exhilaration of being in it more than others, but everyone has one. And the BlindSpots live in there. So if you're going to find them, you have to be willing to go in there too.

You will be motivated to stay comfortable if you don't see much payoff for BlindSpotting or you think your current pattern is temporary. You may choose to stay stuck even when your behavior doesn't produce what you truly want. You think it's safe, secure, and of course, comfortable. As amazing as it sounds, for many people the discomfort of not getting the results they want seems more comfortable than venturing into their DiscomfortZone and hunting for the BlindSpot.

Can you hear Spot barking?

WoofWoof: Fear or resisting discomfort is what makes change so difficult.

(WoofWoof – From now on, we're sure Spot will sound off whenever there is a dot to be connected or a clue to be uncovered as you sharpen your BS detection skills. Listen up.)

1. What is a DiscomfortZone?

   A DiscomfortZone is any place outside of the safe and comfortable physical, psychological, or energetic boundary you have created and seek to maintain.

2. How does a DiscomfortZone form?

   When you're little, people who love you or are responsible for you try to keep you from injuring/ killing yourself through your normal curiosity and sense of adventure. So, they instill FEAR of the unknown, the new, the unsupervised. They close in the boundaries of your exploration and paint a grim picture of what may be waiting for you just over the edge of your (or their) comfort boundary. (It's for your own good and lets them allow you out of their sight once in awhile.) If you do venture into the unknown, the new, or the unsupervised and are caught, you are often reinforced with disapproval or punishment and feel *guilt* or *shame*. (Again, it is for your own good for the next time you're out of their sight contemplating doing something foolish or dangerous.)

3. Is the DiscomfortZone a good idea?

Certainly, when you are a child. You really could be hurt, injured, killed or could hurt, injure, or kill someone or something else. A child may not know the difference between a stuffed toy and a ferocious gorilla. Adults usually do. (Don't you?) So as an adult, your attitude about the DiscomfortZone instilled in childhood – and how you use it now – may need to be revised.

4. How do you know when you're *in* your DiscomfortZone?

We've never met anyone who didn't know they were in there, but just in case, we'll explain. You'll usually experience some level of your automatic biological response: fight or flight. You can experience fight or flight physically, psychologically, or emotionally. (The emotion of fight is anger. The emotion of flight is fear.)

5. What's wrong with fight or flight?

Nothing. As a matter of fact, it's real helpful when there is a real danger. But remember, unless you've taken steps to turn off your AutoPilot, you probably still think a lot of unknown, new, or unsupervised things are dangerous. (You probably know people who just automatically say "No!" to any new idea or situation.) The BlindSpot is there when you don't remember you're choosing. You can choose to be more aware of your automatic danger messages and test their accuracy.

6. What should you know about your DiscomfortZone?

It's always expanding or contracting. Time spent in the DiscomfortZone usually transforms a part of the zone into something rewarding and eventually comfortable. (If you're not stretching into it, the DiscomfortZone is expanding while you're shrinking.)

Many of you mistake the *feelings* you have about entering your DiscomfortZone for your intuition, common sense, rational thinking, or reality. Being uncomfortable and truly in danger are two different things.

7. Should you just ignore your DiscomfortZone?

Absolutely not. (You probably couldn't ignore it even if you tried.) You should thank it for all the times it really has come to your rescue. You must love it for all the ways it has modified your behavior appropriately up to now. Then, you need to let it know that you are back at the controls. AutoPilot is off and *choosing* is on. Exploring your DiscomfortZone can now become an adventure connected with growth and flexibility. It ceases to be an old, unnecessary, automatic limitation based on unreasonable fear of the unknown or the untried or the *uncomfortable*. To master your new skills, you have to be willing to operate at the CounterIntuitive™ level. CounterIntuitive behavior feels odd or uncomfortable precisely because it is new or unusual. This feeling is likely to send you back into your DiscomfortZone. (Welcome home.)

CHAPTER FIVE

You'd Never Die on the Chair, Would You? (How BlindSpots Hide.)

BlindSpots stay hidden:
> because so much of your behavior is unconscious,
> because you ignore or discount verbal feedback from others,
> because you don't even know you need to look for BlindSpots,
> because you're so attached to your patterns you can't imagine there is anything else you could do – or would want to do,
> because you blame others,
> because you think it doesn't matter if you don't look,
> because you're very attached to being right or choke on the thought of having to admit you're wrong,
> because the choices you do see are unappealing,
> because you're too embarrassed when you find a BlindSpot.

Can you hear Spot barking?

WoofWoof: You chose – and continue to choose – your own BlindSpots.

That's a pretty scary thought. Many of you are already calculating the hundreds of reasons BlindSpots have invaded your system like a virus, completely out of your control, or have been given to you like an ugly present by someone else. If you continue to believe either of these explanations, we don't have much to offer you. Perhaps you should get a shot or live in a cave. If you believe your BlindSpots are completely beyond your control, put this book down immediately – there is nothing here for you.

If, on the other hand, you're the least bit curious about how you might contribute to your unproductive patterns or you have an inkling that you're a bigger player in generating BlindSpots than you've been admitting – read on. There is plenty here for you.

Every day of your life you make hundreds of choices. You choose what to wear, what to eat, what to watch on television, who to call on the phone, where to go – the list is endless. Those are all conscious decisions and because they are, you see them clearly as choices. But what about all the unconscious decisions you make throughout the day?

You choose how you are going to respond:
    when your spouse really irritates you.
    when your child won't clean his room.
    when your boss tells you to work late.
    when a driver cuts you off in traffic.

We know these reactions *seem* automatic. They are often instantaneous. But your mind and body, together, is such an amazing bio-computer that although your reactions often appear in a split second, many internal calculations have been made to create the reaction. Don't confuse what seem to be automatic choices with not choosing. On some level, you are still choosing, even though it *seems* as if there is no choice involved.

Your PsychoBiological system is both efficient and confounding. You are constantly refining your beliefs and desires so that you don't have to think through every single reaction. We know we're very happy with a system that quickly gets us on a chair at the sight of a big scorpion crawling down the hall. But we also know people who don't jump on a chair. We've seen people on television (and we don't want to know them) who rush to pick up a scorpion and make friends with it. So lots of choices are available.

The chair-jumping works particularly well for us – so far. This strategy is the result of lots of micro-decisions and carries the full force of our survival commitment. Just notice that somewhere along the way, we hooked evidence together – a bunch of beliefs and choices – to produce and sustain the chair-jumping behavior. It is almost impossible to say what the evidence is, but look at just a few possibilities.

The probable case against the scorpion in support of chair-jumping:

Scorpions are dangerous.
Scorpions are disgusting. (Our sincere apologies to the scorpion-lovers out there.)
Scorpions bite.
Bites hurt and a scorpion bite could kill you. (Yes, we know this isn't true. Not all your evidence is true either.)
When a scorpion is around, the safest place to be is off the floor.
If you're on the chair screaming, someone else will come and take care of the scorpion.

Notice that we don't claim to have the time or inclination to think through this evidence every time a scorpion appears. It is just the background we have put in place over the years which prompts our graceful flight to the furniture. It is now an automatic pattern which, in a nanosecond, we choose to activate every time we see a scorpion. We confess that this pattern is occasionally activated by a leaf that only looks like a scorpion, but better safe than sorry.

It is interesting to note that humans seem to be the only one-trial animal. Humans can activate a pattern once and have it become a habit. We probably locked this whole bug escape routine into our memory banks the very first time we took to chair and successfully saved our lives from a scorpion. It's not a BlindSpot yet, because so far, it is working to get us exactly what we want:

1. a safe distance from scorpions.
2. someone else getting the scorpion out of our environment.

This pattern turns into a BlindSpot when it no longer works and is the only thing we continue to try. It is a BlindSpot when we say, "We can't help it." If we find ourselves alone in a house confronting a scorpion and leap to a chair, we're following the old reliable habit. It is a BlindSpot when the scorpion remains and we're stuck on the chair, thinking this is all we can do. It is definitely a BlindSpot when someone discovers our skeletal remains on the chair because we couldn't find another choice and the scorpion eventually invited his friends and family to watch.

You might be thinking, "How big an idiot would you have to be to die on the chair?" Precisely! Yet we see people symbolically dying on the chair all the time because they don't recognize a BlindSpot, don't recognize it's a choice they've made, and don't do anything differently.

Remember, BlindSpots stay hidden for all kinds of reasons – choices – you perpetuate.

Review the scorpion pattern:

> The behavior is out of our conscious awareness. We don't think twice. We see a scorpion, we jump. As simple as that. And what's your point? Wouldn't you?
>
> We ignore verbal feedback from others. Our husbands have said many times, "What are you going to do if you're home alone? Die on the chair waiting for someone to come along?" How ridiculous! What are they talking about?
>
> We don't even know we need to look at the pattern. We don't see the problem!

We are attached to our patterns. Hey, it works just fine, ok?

We blame others. We haven't even mentioned that if the exterminator did a better job, we wouldn't have to worry about scorpions in the house in the first place. Since they're so incompetent, what are we supposed to do?

We don't know the cost is high. We couldn't imagine ever dying on the chair! How farfetched is that?

We can't admit we're wrong. This is a perfectly good strategy. Enough said!

Other choices are unappealing. What are you suggesting – that we just stay down there on the floor with the scorpion? That we risk a bite? That we take our lives in our hands for no good reason? Are you nuts?

We only see two polar choices: stay on the floor or jump on the chair. You do the math.

We are too embarrassed to find a BlindSpot. Hey, we're professionals! How could this be an unspotted BlindSpot right under our noses (or chairs)?

You can see how it works, even with something as simple and innocuous as a bug pattern. Regardless of the reasons, the evidence, the thoughts, the feelings, we'll stay stuck in that pattern until we have even the tiniest desire to take a look at our hidden choices.

Think about the reasons a BlindSpot stays hidden.

Lack of awareness:
Most of us spend more time than we think on

AutoPilot. When is the last time you drove somewhere in town and couldn't really remember the trip? It's a very common occurrence. People go mindless all the time. If you allow yourself to be persistently mindless about your patterns and their impact, you'll have a hard time unmasking any BlindSpots.

Ignoring verbal feedback from others:
We're not suggesting that you have to pay attention to everything anyone ever says to you. We are suggesting, however, that feedback from a credible source, or feedback that seems familiar, deserves some small bit of your attention. Other people see things you might miss. Other people see your behaviors from a different perspective. As long as you recognize that their feedback is just information which might – or might not – be helpful, you can make use of it in your BlindSpotting.

Not looking:
You may not be able to notice things you're unprepared to see or not curious about finding. Unless you're a natural BlindSpotter or you've had your attention drawn to BlindSpotting, you might continue to think there is nothing going on behind the curtain that you even need to notice. You might even believe that what's in your conscious awareness is all there is. You won't develop a BlindSpotting MindSet™ until you believe there is something behind the curtain. Do you believe?

Pattern attachment:
We just love our patterns. You'd think we were getting a prize or something. We cultivate them,

we nurture them, and we rely on them. You may never have thought that your finely tuned pattern could be getting in your way. And until you think your wonderful patterns might have different sides, you won't discover many BlindSpots.

Blame:

Ahh, the Blindfold of great significance. If you blame, if you're righteous, if you deflect your attention to others and how their shortcomings or behaviors give you little or no choice, it will be impossible to find your BlindSpots. And, indeed, why should you even look? It is *their* fault, after all!

Dismissing cost:

We're amazed at how often people don't ConnectTheDots™ between their choices and patterns and the resulting outcomes. You are probably very clear about the Intention of your behavior or pattern. But how often do you look at what your choices are actually producing?

Remember Nick and the tree limb? Do you think he spent much time thinking, "I'm getting whacked on the head because of a choice I'm making?" Or just imagine Myrtle saying, "I think I'm so exhausted because my patterns aren't very flexible."

Little Alex, on the other hand, was much closer to uncovering his BlindSpot because he was aware that there was a cost. He knew he didn't want to play games with himself because he lied and cheated. Those Dots were Connected. With a little awareness, he was closer to making new choices.

Being right:

Oh how we love to be right. If blame hasn't taken your full quota of righteousness, being right will take the rest. It is so easy to see this BlindSpot if you're outside the event. Just think of all the times you've watched people defend their choices even when they are producing chaos. (Not you, of course.)

Phil's story:

> Phil was driving down a local street several years ago, looked up, and saw another driver headed toward him on his side of the median. He actually heard himself say in his head, "What's the matter with you? Get off my side of the street!" Fortunately, Phil also realized he wasn't getting out of the way. "As I pulled over and saw the other driver flash by, I couldn't believe how righteously indignant I still was. I also couldn't believe I almost didn't pull over. I would have been right – but dead."

We have seen people choose being right over being happy or satisfied or successful so many times. And often when we ask them which they would rather be – right or happy and satisfied – they are incensed they can't have it all. It is often so.

WoofWoof

Can you hear Spot barking?

WoofWoof: Sometimes it is a choice between being right and being happy or creating the impact which matches your Intentions. (Sorry to be the ones to tell you.)

Unappealing choices:

One pattern we see over and over has to do with extremes.

Eric's story:

> Eric was complaining about his job and his boss. He hated both and was stressed all the time. We suggested the possibility that he look for another job. He spat back at us, "Do you want me to live on the street?"

Of course we didn't want him living on the street – unless he wanted to. We were fascinated, but not surprised, to observe how Eric jumped all the way from contemplating another job to living on the street. This PolarJump™ has become a reliable BlindSpot detector for us. When you notice it in your own thinking, can you hear Spot barking? There are hundreds of choices between thinking about another job and the circumstances that would put someone out on the street. However, if you think having the thought leads to street living, you'll never see the BlindSpot and certainly never contemplate that option again. And it will all make perfect sense to you – as every BlindSpot pattern always does until the blindfold disappears.

Embarrassment:

The list of nasty labels people use to describe themselves after uncovering a BlindSpot goes on and on. The basic flavor of the self-talk revolves around "stupid." If you think you're stupid (or worse) for having a BlindSpot or two, trust us, they will hide forever. A BlindSpot about BlindSpots is the belief that BlindSpots are somehow "bad." We suggest you find them interesting, fascinating, and whenever possible, amusing. All of those attitudes seem to coax them out from behind the curtain more consistently than the "stupid!" label. If you're not willing to make friends with your BlindSpots, they will stay hidden. Wouldn't you?

CHAPTER SIX

This Can't Be Right!

Gwen's story:

When Gwen was in college, she took up skiing. A friend of hers arranged for her to have lessons with an excellent ski instructor. During the initial practice, the instructor, Lars, proved to be patient and competent. She trusted his abilities and was progressing quite well on flat snow. It wasn't long before he suggested they go "up the mountain." She was willing. She had done everything he'd told her to do so far and it had all worked out just fine.

As they hopped off the chair lift, Lars pointed to the route back down the mountain. It was labeled the "beginners' run," but to Gwen it looked like a sheer drop off the side of the mountain. Lars positioned them at the top of the hill. "Hill" is what he called it, while Gwen was already referring to it in her mind as the "cliff."

Lars smiled at Gwen and reminded her to "lean into the downhill ski." This procedure hadn't gotten her full attention when they practiced it on a flat surface. From the top of this cliff, leaning out into nothing with the possibility . . . make that probability in her mind . . . of tumbling over and rolling down the mountain to her death seemed like a really stupid thing to do.

But she trusted Lars to be telling her the right thing to do and pushed off. Everything in her body was screaming, "Don't lean out you idiot . . . you'll be killed." So, even with the best of intentions, she pulled back. The laws of skiing physics were now engaged. Gwen cut a diagonal path across the hill at what felt like 90 miles an hour and crashed into some trees.

Her hat flew off, her glasses flew off, and she was sure she'd separated some muscles connecting her ribs. As she lay there dazed, Lars swooshed up to her and calmly inquired, "Excuse me Gwen. Do you know which is your downhill ski?"

All she could do was squeak out a feeble, "Uh huh," and try to get up.

Again they positioned themselves at the top of the hill. "The downhill ski," Lars reminded her, giving the appropriate ankle a little dink for effect with his ski pole. She really meant to lean into the downhill ski. But, as before, her brain dramatically pointed out to her that "This can't be right! You'll be killed!" Her body heard the warning, pulled back, and Gwen ended up in the trees on the other side of the trail.

After the third time, when Lars was looking at her like he was sure she couldn't tell downhill from uphill, Gwen came to a conclusion lying in the trees. She was going to die on the mountain no matter what. She would either continue to disintegrate her skeletal structure in the trees or tumble to her doom after leaning into the downhill ski. She decided to get it over with.

She stood far enough away from Lars so that he couldn't dink her ankle again and pushed off. No matter what, she was going to lean into the downhill ski and put herself out of her misery. So she did.

And miraculously, she was skiing. She had no grace or style, but she was navigating under control across the path. She was so amazed it worked that she had to stop. Lars swooshed up to her again yelling, "Keep going, you've got it now! You finally figured out which is your downhill ski." She didn't bother to tell him that she'd known all along, but just couldn't believe it would work until she was resigned to her death.

It is those CounterIntuitive moments that allow you to look for, identify, and ultimately redesign your BlindSpots. Sometimes the behavior that seems the most wrong is actually the most right.

Believing too much in the correctness of how something feels can confuse you. You've probably said at some point, "I just followed my intuition." We're big fans of intuition and believe it exists. We also know that it is hard to tell the difference between real intuition and habitual unconscious responses until you've embraced CounterIntuitive alternatives. Until you've tried a new pattern – even when it feels so wrong – you have no access to a new, potentially more productive perspective.

Willingness to behave CounterIntuitively means going ahead even when your brain is saying, "This can't be right." Caution: We don't mean doing something foolhardy or life-threatening. However, we'll warn you that sometimes you *think* a new behavior is life-threatening when it really isn't. (Remember Eric who thought considering another job would automatically put him out on the street? Remember Gwen who thought the downhill ski would be her demise?) It just feels that way because it is inside your DiscomfortZone. And you remember how weird things are in there.

Your CounterIntuitive choices come into focus as you imagine going to a swimming party when you're afraid to get into the water. You see people having fun in the pool, but getting into the pool just doesn't feel safe. When you're encouraged by friends to "jump in," you think they've lost their minds. You might dip your toe into the water, but going in is out of the question. Then the party is over. You never entered the pool – even at the shallow end. You missed all the fun your friends had. You missed the fact that they were safe in the water. The CounterIntuitive feeling you labeled "unsafe" was simply your DiscomfortZone. There is no completely accurate way to determine what it's like in the pool until you're in the pool.

Contemplating CounterIntuitive behavior usually produces discomfort – that feeling before you jump into the pool. Some discomfort may be found in every Spot of a BlindSpotting investigation. There will be countless moments where you're unsure how it will feel if you commit to a new behavior. You can't know for sure what it will be like or how it will work until you actually do it. The thoughts that keep you stuck may sound like:

"Why open that can of worms?"

"Don't rock the boat. You'll be sorry."
"It can't possibly make that much difference."
"This will never work."
"It's going to be terrible, stupid, embarrassing,
    or worse."

The truth is, you can't possibly know what will result from BlindSpotting and engaging new behavior or how you'll feel until you actually do it – until you trust that something behind the curtain might be getting in your way – until you lean into the downhill ski, or jump in the pool.

Reminder: This is not about engaging harmful behavior. This is about learning to realistically discern the difference between real danger and simple discomfort. It is about recognizing that you often avoid potentially productive behaviors because you let yourself be so sure you know what will happen if you engage these behaviors. As a famous sports manufacturer pointed out, sometimes you have to just do it.

CHAPTER SEVEN

How *Blind* is a BlindSpot?

Mary's Story:

Mary was fortunate enough to have her mother for 40 years of her life. There were many things Mary remembered about her mother and she was reminiscing about them to her friend, Nan, as they packed up her mother's things.

Nan turned from the linen closet and said, "Mary, look at this. Your mother had over a dozen deodorants and 20 cans of hair spray. She really believed in buying in bulk."

"I know," said Mary. "She must have had 16 wooden spoons and 30 of the same plastic bowls in the kitchen. I remember she always had lots of stuff and would say to me that she never wanted to run out of things. I think it is so cute and quirky."

"Quirky?" responded Nan.

"Yes, quirky," Mary said. "I've never understood it, but I thought it was a very entertaining pattern of hers."

Nan looked at Mary with a raised eyebrow and queried, "Do you know you do the same thing?"

"What same thing?" Mary demanded.

"The same collection thing. You must have six cases of toilet paper in your garage, and I believe you have even more wooden spoons than your mother," responded Nan.

Mary stopped for a minute looking a little dazed and then said, "Oh my gosh, I do that don't I? I never noticed."

This is not an unusual occurrence. Many people we observe are quite amused – and sometimes annoyed – by the "quirky" patterns of others, only to find out that they replicate the very same patterns without ever knowing it.

Mary was over 40 years old and had obviously been "buying in bulk" herself for many years. But all she could see was her mother's idiosyncrasy. Her own pattern had been at her fingertips all along, but she never noticed it until someone else pointed it out. Mary was quick to realize that she did have the same pattern as her mother. Some people don't own up to their own patterns so easily.

We're sure you've heard people complain about someone else. (If you haven't, welcome back to Earth. Did you have a nice trip?) And often, you may notice the person doing the complaining exhibits the same pattern that so annoys them. To them the duplication of behavior is invisible, yet it is easy for you to spot – as long as it's someone else's mirror reflection.

That's one of the tricky characteristics of a BlindSpot. Hardly anyone else is blind to yours and you can definitely see patterns in others while they remain clueless.

Can you hear Spot barking?

WoofWoof: Don't think we're telling you to become the BlindSpots Police for all your friends and neighbors. No un-initiated BlindSpotter appreciates having anyone shove their nose into their BlindSpots. It's not invited. It isn't appreciated. It doesn't work.

But, for your own benefit, you could start to pay attention to patterns you're noticing in others. It is highly probable that patterns in others that amuse, annoy, or activate you may be found in your own repertoire. It's possible you're seeing a little thumbnail sketch of your own behavior – a reflection in the mirror. We're just suggesting that you be willing to look.

Because Spot is very *blind.*

BlindSpots – Section TWO

BlindSpots Spotting Strategy

Now you know *what* you're looking, listening, or feeling for, but you still may be unsure how to go about spotting. This section is full of strategies for noticing, uncovering, revealing, and highlighting BlindSpots. Any and all strategies may be useful to you, depending on your interest and current desire.

CHAPTER EIGHT

What Do I Do?

Ok. So now you know about BlindSpots. And you may have admitted to yourself that you might have them. You probably would like to know how to find them, and of course, eventually know what to do with them.

If you're looking for the most productive place to start, look at your MindSet. A MindSet is a blueprint you've created of your beliefs and perspectives. You always operate out of a MindSet – whether you're aware of it or not. Making your MindSets consciously available for self-examination is a core BlindSpot strategy.

Just because you haven't consciously thought about MindSets doesn't mean they don't exist. Nor does it mean MindSets are fixed or unchangeable. Up to now your MindSets have probably been completely automatic and invisible, just like the BlindSpots they may produce.

David's Story:

David took a business class last spring. Everyone was in place and waiting for the instructor to begin when two serious looking people stepped into the classroom and asked to speak to Gretchen Smith and Theodore Townsend. David thought there was going to be trouble, while his colleague Bob elbowed him and said with a grin, "I bet it's their birthday."

While Bob was waiting for the strangers to direct the class in a chorus of "Happy Birthday to You," the two outsiders walked over to the people who'd been identified, leaned over, spoke to them in hushed tones, and escorted them out of the room.

David thought they'd gotten in trouble. Bob suggested they were being taken out for cake.

What you've just read demonstrates different MindSets. We're guessing, but it appears that David's MindSet might have been:

> Just like it was for me in elementary school, being identified in class means trouble.

On the other hand, Bob appears to have had lots of experience with parties and celebrations and appeared to have the MindSet:

> If someone comes for you, it's a party.

It doesn't matter what was really happening when the pair was escorted out of the room. What you're seeing is that the MindSet becomes the lens or filter through which we evaluate and interpret situations. The MindSet creates the differing interpretations of the same event. Based on your MindSet and what it prompts you to think, you automatically generate behaviors and responses that make up your automatic patterns. David was apprehensive, while Bob was excited and a little disappointed he hadn't been invited for cake too.

MindSets are important because they are the source of our automatics – automatic assessments, automatic behaviors, automatic choices. Once you know a person's MindSet, you can be surprisingly accurate in predicting what they may say or do or feel. Knowing your own MindSets enables you to intervene with a strategy before an automatic reaction or response takes place. You can either adjust your MindSet or change your thinking to reevaluate your MindSet. Revealing your own MindSets to yourself is a highly productive challenge.

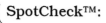 SpotCheck™:

(A SpotCheck is an ongoing shift in your perspective. Once identified, it needs to be attended to regularly until you've expanded the way you once saw things.)

Be willing to notice your own MindSets.

Drew's story:

Drew had gotten on a crowded bus. The aisle was packed and as he squeezed past the first few rows of jammed seats, someone pushed him from behind . . . really hard. Drew is not a violent guy, but he's also not the type to put up with someone being such a jerk. So he turned around, fully armed with righteous indignation, ready to ask whoever pushed him just what the hell he thought he was doing.

As Drew turned around, teeth clenched and ready for anything, he saw that a little old

59

gentleman had dropped his cane and stumbled against him while trying to pick it up.

Drew immediately felt like a jerk himself. He'd been ready to breathe fire in the face of the person who shoved him. When he realized it was this tiny, frail old man, Drew picked up his cane for him, rode with him to his next stop, and helped him off the bus. Drew felt a bit less guilty for wanting to punch the little old man as he made sure he was safely on his way.

Drew's story demonstrates how a shift in information changed a whole response pattern and engaged a completely different MindSet. As you start to notice similar shifts in your own experiences, you'll also notice how important the MindSet is in generating the new behaviors you desire. New information disrupts the same old automatic behaviors inside your BlindSpots.

Most uninitiated BlindSpotters wait for new information to present itself – and even then, may ignore it. It's something different to wonder what new information might be available if you intentionally and prescriptively look for it.

Remember, BlindSpots will hide if:
  you aren't motivated to see them.
  you are avoiding your DiscomfortZone.
  you are ready to pounce on the BlindSpot
    with judgment and shame.
  your ego is in the way because you need to
    be right.
  you have no curiosity about how you get
    yourself stuck.
  you don't know you are stuck.

Can you hear Spot barking?

WoofWoof: Consciously decide you're ready to spot BlindSpots today.

To make change more accessible, we suggest you personalize the BlindSpots and invite them in. They're all named Spot (how handy), they're all friendly, and given the appropriate invitation and environment – they're really anxious to be found.

So how do you look for Spot? SpotDoctorsRx™. We'll be identifying specific SpotDoctor prescriptions from here on out.

Symptom: You want to find a BlindSpot.
SpotDoctorsRx:
Develop a strategy to consciously prepare yourself for this discovery.

Remember that everyone has BlindSpots, so there is nothing disgraceful about spotting one. As a matter of fact, it is a demonstration of courage and commitment to self-improvement every time you begin the BlindSpot hunt. So give yourself a little pat on the back every time you're willing to search.

Remind yourself that BlindSpots are BlindSpots. If you could see them from your normal perspective or with your regular awareness, you would have already seen them. So in some way, you have to look at things differently if you're going to discover a BlindSpot. Spot is very clever, but more friendly than you've imagined. With practice, Spot will be a cooperative partner in your search.

Symptom: I can't Spot my Spots.
SpotDoctorsRx:
To find Spot you are going to be practicing CounterIntuitive thinking, changing your perspective, and finding a host of alternative ways of perceiving your environment so that the BlindSpots' camouflage can melt away.

Decide not to take yourself so seriously. This decision will let you be amused when any BlindSpot appears. A light touch and some laughter are like dog treats for Spot. He may eventually pop from behind the curtain and into view with only the offer of an amused greeting. Cultivate your

amused, curious, and inviting
BlindSpot greetings.

And when Spot is not cooperating (sometimes he won't), practice patience. Spots aren't trained overnight. So be prepared to continue to practice being ready. Sometimes Spot is just waiting to see if you're really serious about all this before he pops out.

Get ready to be surprised – to even be surprised about the way you're being surprised. Once you hook up with Spot, things will not be the same. So, be ready for a change. And be ready to appreciate the change, even when it's not the one you wanted or thought you'd experience. Actually, the bigger the surprise, the better. If you're not surprised, you're probably doing things the same old way and Spot will continue to be invisible. And you'll continue to get what you've always gotten.

If that's ok with you, it's ok with us . . .

CHAPTER NINE

How Spot-Savvy are You?

It's time to give yourself a beginner's report card. As you were reading Section One, how often did you spot the BlindSpot before we explained it? If you were one step ahead of us for every story, give yourself an A+ and notice that you probably already have spotted some of your own Spots – even if you haven't done anything about them yet.

If you started to see a BlindSpot part way through the stories, give yourself an A or A-, depending on your consistency. You're ready to become a reliable and effective BlindSpotter. Spot has just been waiting for your call.

If you read the explanation of BlindSpots in the stories and smacked yourself on the forehead exclaiming, "Of course," as the BlindSpot came into focus, give yourself a solid B. You can spot Spot if you're paying attention.

If, after our explanation, you read the story again and things came into focus, you can award yourself a C or C+. You're an average uninitiated BlindSpotter.

You can see, but it takes work, desire and practice. Prepare to improve.

Go no lower than a C. Even if you think you don't yet deserve a C, you do. You're still reading this book. We suspect there are some clueless pseudo-BlindSpotters out there who were so confused by our stories and unable to Connect any Dots that they've tossed the book aside and Spot buried it in the backyard. Just notice that you're not one of the clueless.

Giving yourself full credit for what you can do – and do do – is very appealing to Spot. Spot knows that if you acknowledge your abilities, they expand. Now, you know it too.

SpotCheck™:

Notice how often you acknowledge yourself or avoid acknowledging yourself when you take a small step forward.

CHAPTER TEN

If You're Behind Me, I Can't Move

Dick's story:

Clair and her husband, Dick, are both therapists and have an office attached to the house where both see clients. Dick usually sees his clients in the late afternoon or evening while Clair sees hers in the morning and early afternoon.

Dick parks his car in front of the house and Clair parks hers in the garage. If any clients park in the driveway, Clair cannot get the car out of the garage. So, for months, she reminded Dick to ask his clients to park in the street.

"One day I had a particularly important appointment away from the house and when I opened the garage door, there was one of Dick's clients parked right behind my car. I had to interrupt the session to ask his client to move it," Clair explained.

The next day, after one of his clients left, Dick came into the office and said, "Your client was parked in the driveway." Clair noticed he was a little snippy, but thought he might just be tired. So, she just told him it was ok.

Well, snippy turned to snappy and Dick snarled, "Ok. Why do your clients get to park in the driveway and mine don't? That really seems like a double standard!"

We're giving you a moment here to think about Dick's question. Yes, this is a test. Read no further until you hear your brain say, "Oh!"

We understand that Clair was unable to stifle her laughter, which didn't make Dick one bit happy. Did you figure it out yet?

"Dick," Clair said, still giggling, "think about it. Why can my clients park in the driveway and yours can't?"

Dick looked annoyed and perplexed. "Why?" he continued to snarl.

"Why would I need to get my car out of the garage when I'm with a client?" Clair said, as patiently as she could.

Dick made a couple of false starts at responding and then finally said, sheepishly, "Oh, sorry. I wasn't looking at it that way."

Believing that he wasn't being treated fairly, Dick was completely blind to the obvious. Clair and Dick have a long history of helping each other find BlindSpots – his, hers, and theirs. So this little conversation was pretty efficient and ended with them both laughing. As you might imagine, it could have gone very differently had Dick's BlindSpot remained *blind*.

We have watched Clair tell that story many times. Almost no one fails to grasp the logic and the obvious immediately. Eyes widen, mouths drop ever so slightly open, and you can almost hear the thought, "Duh!"

In all fairness to Dick, this moment is no more invisible to Dick or more visible to others than most BlindSpots. It's always easier for you to see all of Spot when he's not licking *your* face. On a regular basis, we are all in the middle of something where we remain clueless while others around us are amused and/or annoyed by our *blindness*.

Accepting that Spot is blin*d* – really blin*d* – can motivate you to explore your own limited vision or paradigm. Accepting the fact that how you see things is not always accurate or complete may trigger a search for a BlindSpot before someone else pokes your nose in it. Believe us, it's far less embarrassing to begin to Spot your own BlindSpots.

SpotCheck™:

Be willing to notice when your version of what's going on is completely different from another person's. (Don't get nervous. We're a long way from suggesting that you change your mind or adopt a new perspective. For now, just see if you are able to notice and pay attention to all the automatic behaviors, thoughts, and feelings that come up if you find discrepancies.)

> Be willing to consider that your perspective may be inaccurate. (Take it easy. Just consider it. Nothing is carved in stone here.)

> Be willing to consider another perspective. (Spot should be growling if you find you can't even imagine any other perspective than the one you have.)

This SpotCheck seems simple. It is. If it sounds easy, it isn't. You are marching right into the heart of your DiscomfortZone and addressing the possibility that you might not always be accurate in how you see things – even when you're sure you're right. Yes, this could be the scary part.

CHAPTER ELEVEN

How Stubborn is Stubborn?

Bebe's Story:

Donna's sister Bebe frequently talked to herself. She didn't wander around muttering under her breath, but had completely quiet conversations in her own head. Bebe often thought she'd talked out loud when she hadn't. Donna had learned to live with – and anticipate – the fact Bebe would tell her she'd said something Donna knew Bebe didn't say, or insist that she'd said something that Donna knew she hadn't. It was just Bebe.

What was mystifying to Donna was that no matter how many times someone told Bebe she had conversations with herself that she thought she had out loud, she refused to believe it.

Donna and Bebe were standing in a group of people at a party when Elliott asked Bebe a question. Everyone turned to Bebe, who said nothing. Elliott said, "Well?" And Bebe replied, "I said I don't really know anything about that."

Elliott looked puzzled and asked, "What do you mean, you said that? You didn't say anything."

Bebe, in her usual fashion, adamantly repeated, "I most certainly did. I said I didn't know anything about it." Elliott, who was looking more confused by the minute, said, "Bebe, your lips didn't even move," and looked to the group for confirmation. Everyone cheerfully supported Elliott murmuring, "That's right, no lips moved."

Bebe, intractable to the last, actually said, "I don't care if my lips moved or not, I said I didn't know anything about it! Case closed!"

Well, everyone burst into laughter, even her sister Donna. Eight witnesses to lips not moving and sound not uttered impressed Bebe not one bit. She had said what she said and no amount of witness testimony was going to change her mind.

This is stubborn. This is a failure to contemplate even the most remote possibility that what you're so sure is happening may not be what's happening at all. Since everyone in Bebe's family knew she talked in her head, it seldom produced problems. Bebe didn't know Elliott and probably would never see him again, so his opinion or reaction wasn't a real problem for her either.

However, you can see the potential for problems – even disaster – in Bebe's life if this pattern remains hidden from her. And it will, as long as she stubbornly fails to consider the feedback she receives from others.

Who knows why Bebe is so stubborn about not considering other people's feedback? But we're going to guess you might have an example in your own life where stubbornness keeps you from looking behind the curtain.

Stubbornness can be good. We want someone stubbornly committed to helping us. We want someone stubbornly honest or considerate. But, like anything else about automatic patterns, having no flexibility will slam you into a BlindSpot every time. And keep you stuck there indefinitely.

How stubborn is stubborn? Pretty darn stubborn!

SpotCheck™:

Be willing to notice consistent feedback when it hits critical mass. (We don't mean that everything everyone tells you is true. We don't mean you have to consider all feedback from any source. We are suggesting that if you keep hearing the same thing from several different people – especially if you strongly disagree – it would be productive to identify it for a SpotCheck.)

Be willing to be curious about what all the other people are seeing or experiencing that you're not.

Be willing to consider that you have some behavior lurking behind the curtain that could be a potential BlindSpot.

This SpotCheck seems simple. It is. If it sounds easy, it isn't. You are marching right into the heart of your DiscomfortZone and addressing the possibility that you might not always be accurate in how you see things, even when you're sure you're right. Yes, we know we've said this before. And we'll be saying it again.

CHAPTER TWELVE

Let Go of That Belt!

Dwayne's story:

Lisa's husband, Dwayne, had a brown belt. She believed he might have inherited it from his great grandfather – at least it seemed that old to Lisa. Dwayne wore it with everything, including black pants. It was frayed, stained, and cracked. He loved that belt.

Because he had, as he put it, "a completely serviceable belt," he saw no need to purchase a new one in any color.

When Lisa and Dwayne went shopping with their friends, Sam and Judith, and happened into a men's clothing store, Lisa spotted a lovely black belt and took it to Dwayne. "Try this on. It's really handsome and would go so nicely with your black pants," she said.

"I don't need another belt. The one I have on is perfectly fine," said Dwayne. Hoping she might influence him with others' opinions, Lisa asked Sam and Judith, both snappy dressers, what they thought of the new black belt. Sam replied, "That's a nice belt, Dwayne." And Judith, who isn't shy, lifted Dwayne's tee shirt to look at the one he had on. She shrieked, "That's disgusting. Where did you get that awful thing?"

"What's wrong with my belt?" scowled Dwayne. "It's disgusting," repeated Judith as she started to take it off him. "Look at it. How long have you had it? Where did you get it? Good grief, you have a brown belt on with black pants. Who let you out of the house like this?" Judith fired at Dwayne.

All but Dwayne were in hysterics at this little scene, as Dwayne pushed Judith away and babbled about his wonderful brown belt.

Finally Sam said sheepishly, "Dwayne, that belt you're wearing is pretty ratty. Why don't you let your wife buy you a new one if she wants?" With his buddy caving, Dwayne finally relented. As Lisa paid for the belt, the salesman said, "Sir, would you like to wear your new belt?"

Everyone chimed in with encouragement for Dwayne to wear the new black belt with his black pants. Once again he gave in. "Would you like me to dispose of the other belt for you, sir?" the salesman asked, holding the tattered brown thing at arm's length like a dead snake. You would have thought he just offered to cut off Dwayne's hand. "Absolutely not," Dwayne roared. "Just put it in the bag with my receipt."

"What are you going to do with that ratty old belt?" Judith squealed. "Just never mind," said Dwayne, snatching his belt and heading for the door.

"Later that evening as we were getting ready to have dinner with Judith and Sam, Dwayne came out of the closet," Lisa explained. "He was

75

very handsome in his black trousers, attractive collarless shirt, black loafers and . . . I couldn't believe my eyes. He was wearing his ratty brown belt."

When Lisa asked him why, all he could say – rather pitifully – was, "I love this belt."

Whether or not Dwayne deserved to keep his ratty brown belt or wear it with his black pants is certainly a debatable issue. But Dwayne's attachment to an old, well-used article of clothing which didn't match anything else he was wearing sounds suspiciously like our attachments to old, obsolete patterns. If you are unable to throw away the symbolic ratty brown belts in your life or commit to wearing new black belts that match your clothing, you may just be stuck – out of sentiment or habit – in patterns that no longer work.

SpotCheck™:

Be willing to notice any and all patterns that have you hanging on to anything. (We're not saying hanging on to things is a bad habit in and of itself. Sometimes, it's really good to hang on to things. You want to hang on to this book, right? You just want to be able to notice what you hang on to – whether it's a tattered old belt, a non-productive belief, a hurtful pattern, righteousness, or a BlindSpot – so you can decide to keep it, revise it, or throw it away.)

Be willing to look at what you've discovered and ask yourself how well it is working. (You had a very good reason for holding on to whatever you discover. That reason is likely to be quite old and, perhaps, outmoded. You'll never know until you look.)

Be willing to consider the cost of what you've discovered – to yourself and those around you. (We can almost guarantee that if you've thought about what you're holding on to at all, it has usually been to reinforce how right you were to hold tight. Going to the next step – assessing cost – may be very revealing.)

This SpotCheck doesn't sound so easy – and it probably won't be. You're venturing into unknown territory and examining results that you may never have considered before. You're still in the DiscomfortZone, but if you're curious, it may be more interesting than intimidating.

CHAPTER THIRTEEN

You Can't Get to D Without A, B, and C.

Ann's story:

Abel's wife, Ann, is definitely the computer genius in the family. He feels he can hold his own with their six-year old, but he's happy Ann is around to help when the computer acts up.

They had just installed a new computer program at the office. Ann had the same program on her home computer. Abel had a little tutoring, but was still unsure of how to do things. He opened a program, got about halfway into the application, and was stumped. He immediately called Ann and asked for her help.

He told her exactly where he was in the program and she said, "Ok, re-start your computer."

Abel asked if she was sure and explained again where he was in the process. "Yes, yes," Ann said. "Just re-start the computer."

Abel re-started the computer and Ann directed him, step by step, through the program from the beginning. About five minutes later,

they were exactly where Abel had been when
he called Ann in the first place.
"Hey, wait a minute," Abel said. "This is
where I was when I called. Why couldn't we have
just started from there?" Ann patiently
explained, "You have to start from the beginning."
"Couldn't you just start from where I was
and go from there?" Abel asked. Ann replied,
"Do you want my help or not? You have to start
at the beginning and that's that!"

For Ann, there was clearly one procedure. There's
nothing wrong with having a procedure, unless it's
your only one, or you don't know it's your only one,
or you can't even contemplate another one. Most of
us don't think twice about all the routines we have
built into our system to make us efficient. You don't
have to think when you've engaged a habit or rote
procedure. Remember Congress and those buckets
of ice? Remember Myrtle who had to stay up because
her bed was already made? And remember Ann, who
had to start with step one – all the time?

Knowing that mindless patterns may be a source of
BlindSpots should encourage you to explore how many
you have and how automatically they are engaged.

Even more important, you might want to be curious
about how your patterns reflect your flexibility – or
lack of it. How easy is it for you to change from what
you're used to or from what feels most comfortable?
How quickly can you even think of another way of
responding to a situation? Versatility and flexibility
are strong antidotes for BlindSpots. If flexibility comes
to you naturally, good for you. If you are flexibly
challenged, it is something you will want to address.

79

Even if you think flexibility comes to you naturally, ask around. You may find that you're flexible when you're flexible and when you're not flexible – *blind.*

SpotCheck:

Be willing to notice the things you can only do one way.

Be willing to notice the things you never thought could be done another way.

Be willing to get curious about how other people do the same thing you do but in a different way.

Be willing to notice how unbelievably comfortable it is to do things the way you always do them and how really annoying it may be to attempt to do them any other way.

Be willing to see that you might not be as flexible as you can be – that perhaps you've gotten very set in your ways and your brain could stand some unlocking.

This SpotCheck will tax your creativity, which may be entertaining for some of you and frustrating for others. This is a great place to determine how you really feel about learning and doing things another way. If you always felt stupid in school when the teacher moved on to something you didn't know, this SpotCheck will bump into that BlindSpot. Addressing that BlindSpot will open the door to many productive and new perspectives, which you only reach through your DiscomfortZone.

BlindSpots — Section THREE

I Think I've Spotted One! Now What?

When you think you have discovered a BlindSpot, there are a variety of strategic steps, depending on your perspective of the moment.

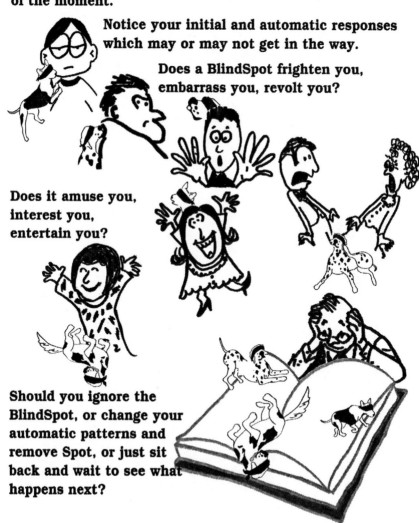

Notice your initial and automatic responses which may or may not get in the way.

Does a BlindSpot frighten you, embarrass you, revolt you?

Does it amuse you, interest you, entertain you?

Should you ignore the BlindSpot, or change your automatic patterns and remove Spot, or just sit back and wait to see what happens next?

CHAPTER FOURTEEN

Not So Fast . . .

Eldon's story:

Eldon was curious about everything – particularly himself – and was used to lots of introspection. He thought he knew just about everything that made him tick. When introduced to the concept of BlindSpots in one of our workshops, he quickly became intrigued. As he applied his usual dedication throughout the workshop, he began to discover that people saw him as more serious than he thought he was and they seemed to not always consider him part of the group.

Eldon also started to realize that he didn't disclose much information about himself, leaving a lot of blanks to be filled in by others. He was curious about the fact that so many blanks seemed to be filled in with what he considered inaccurate perceptions about himself.

The result of Eldon's current behaviors was that he didn't quite fit in with his peers and they didn't consider him completely "one of the guys." Eldon realized he didn't like feeling on the outside.

When we asked Eldon what he wanted, he told us he wanted to fit in. He wanted to be more a part of his work team, wanted people to know him better, and wanted them to realize he was funny.

Eldon decided this whole pattern was producing conditions he did not want, so he asked for some strategic help in modifying his newly discovered BlindSpot. We suggested he begin his investigation by determining how willing he really was to change his beliefs and behaviors.

Eldon, a highly motivated learner, immediately said, "Of course I'm willing. That's why I'm here."

Not so fast . . .

Our experience has shown us over and over that people think they are far more willing to change their BlindSpot patterns than they actually are. It's like those people who claim to love change until they're presented with a change they don't like. So take time to determine how the automatic pattern came to be. Determine what the pattern may have been designed to accomplish. Determine what the pattern *truly* accomplishes. You will reveal how willing you are to adjust or how willing you are to release what's in the way of the BlindSpots transformation.

In Eldon's case, he made a decision early in life to "play it close to the vest." He chose early on to intentionally create blanks and keep people guessing. Eldon realized his father had been like that. Eldon had always considered his father an extremely interesting and intelligent man. He told us he had several wonderful mentors and role models for success in school and business. "The really smart ones," he told us, "didn't give away much. They were always hard to figure out." His early decision continued to be confirmed and reinforced.

Eldon admitted he thought he and the "really smart ones" were better than other people. And he liked that. He was actually proud of feeling superior to almost everyone. He had always thought he was so successful in work because of these patterns. We realized it might be harder for Eldon to modify his patterns than he initially thought, since it meant adjusting his "better-than" thoughts. It also might mean finding other ways to feel like one of the guys without sacrificing his business success.

Eldon was stuck between two polar possibilities, a familiar place for the SpotDoctors. He had done a great job of identifying and investigating a BlindSpot. He'd uncovered beliefs he had held unconsciously for a long time. But he told us he found himself in a position where he thought there were only two options:

> If he continued to revel in feeling superior to other people and continued his enigmatic behaviors, he thought it guaranteed on-going success – and he wanted to be successful.

> **OR**

> If he decided to be more forthcoming and modify his need for superiority in some way, he might be sacrificing his tried and true formula for success, just to be seen as one of the guys. But he also wanted to be one of the guys.

Conflict like this between two different Intentions, especially when you see only two polar possibilities, is a classic BlindSpot. It can be a huge SpeedBump on the road to willingness to change.

We left Eldon in the middle of this conflict, grappling with his willingness to adjust his attachment to superiority, knowing that something about that perspective would have to change or the behaviors he wanted to change would not follow – or stick. We left him to investigate his beliefs and fully understand his two polar choices. More important, we challenged him to imagine some options between the poles. We could tell by the look on his face that the latter suggestion sounded completely unattainable. He asked us, "What other options could there possibly be?" His words didn't say, "You idiots, you," but his tone certainly did. We sent him away with one of our very successful and very simple prescriptions.

Symptom: You can't Spot your Spots.
SpotDoctorsRx:
Go away and think about it. Let yourself percolate.

So Eldon went off to percolate the important information he'd accumulated by venturing this far into his DiscomfortZone.

Imagine our surprise and delight to find Eldon in another of our workshops a year later. We were anxious to see how he had progressed with the patterns he wanted to change. Amazingly, Eldon once again revealed he was still working on the same BlindSpot and hadn't gotten very far in the process. In fact, we saw he had changed nothing. He then asked again, "So, what do I do?"

We asked him what he now thought about needing to feel superior to other people. He said, "I still like feeling superior." We reminded him that his attachment to being better than other people was really interfering with the changes he thought he wanted. We reminded him it is hard to be one of the guys when he prided himself on being superior. So once again, we suggested he investigate his true willingness to modify the beliefs that generated all the behaviors he wanted to change.

To Eldon's credit, he squinted his eyes and said, "There's something here I'm still not seeing, right?" That is exactly what a BlindSpot is – something in the way that can't be seen – yet. So once again, Eldon wandered off to percolate, thinking he was fully willing and dedicated to bringing Spot around.

Can you hear Spot barking?

WoofWoof: Some BlindSpots take a lot of patience.

Six months after that workshop, we received an e-mail from Eldon. He said he'd been doing a lot of thinking and was now ready to move.

Yes, we had heard this from Eldon before. He claimed to be completely willing. Could we just tell him some simple things to do which would help other people see him as one of the guys? We exchanged a few e-mails inquiring about his better-than beliefs, only to discover that Eldon was still very attached to the belief that he was better than almost anyone.

We admit that we were amused.

We have great sympathy and admiration for anyone who struggles to unmask a BlindSpot. But other people's BlindSpots and seeing where they get stuck are also amusing to us. We confess we're not so amused when we're the ones who are stuck. We suspect you may find the same thing.

But enough about us. Poor Eldon was right back at the same spot where we'd left him the last time he asked the same question. Eldon continued to ask what he could DO differently. But his willingness to do anything differently was still tied up in his belief system. How could he generate any real "one of the guys" behavior when he was so attached to not being one of the guys and simultaneously so attached to always being better than any of the guys?

You're seeing the BlindSpot inside the BlindSpot – a double-decker SpeedBump. Your inner beliefs, the thoughts they produce, and the behaviors they generate will overwhelm any changes that are inconsistent with the core belief. So in order to permanently adjust to new behavior – which produces a new result – the belief that impedes that behavior must be addressed. And if you're caught in a polar conflict – seemingly choosing between being one of the guys and continuing to be successful – you won't budge, at least not in the way you want to budge.

Eldon was stuck wanting to behave differently without giving up his attachment to feeling superior to other people. He was also afraid that if he modified his need to feel superior, he would sacrifice success. It's a catch-22 – a big one. Spot could spend the rest of his life chasing his tail on this one and end up exactly where he started.

The blocking effect of such conflict validates the importance of the question, "Are you willing?" It is often why the quick "yes" is not really accurate – yet.

Ask yourself if you are willing to examine all parts of the BlindSpot and address the really sticky parts that threaten to gum up your whole BlindSpots project. That often means letting go of a belief you hold dear because there is simply no way to crawl over it, tunnel under it, or sneak around it on the way to new behavior. It also may mean seriously expanding your creativity to discover the many options that may be found between the polar results you invented.

Every now and then we hear from Eldon. He always asks the same thing. "Give me a few simple behaviors to help me be more one of the guys." And we take him right back to the core each time. Eldon is always willing to introduce new behaviors he thinks will change everything.

During one of our workshops, Eldon, in some frustration, approached us and asked, "Can't I just smile more? That would be a good strategy, wouldn't it?"

We're always supportive of any change someone is willing to attempt. So we said, "Fine. Try smiling more today. And ask a few people in class to keep an eye on you and tell you if you appear to be more a part of the group." He said he would and we promised to check back with him later in the day.

We didn't see Eldon smiling any more than normal. When we asked him what other people had told him during the afternoon, he declared in a rather shocked tone, "They didn't see me smiling more. They didn't think I was any different than I normally am. I don't get it. I thought I was smiling all the time."

We asked Eldon what he'd been thinking during the extended group discussion. Like most people, he immediately claimed he didn't know what he was thinking. We asked him to look more closely, gave him a minute to reflect, and we watched him blush.

"I was thinking what complete idiots these people are. They were saying some of the dumbest things I'd ever heard."

"And did you feel superior to them?" we asked, pretty sure of the answer from the way he still glowed a vibrant pink.

"Of course I did. I was downright smug."

"Feeling and thinking as you did would certainly make a smile hard to access, don't you think?"

Eldon was beginning to see how his need to feel superior and his accompanying judgments would fail to motivate even simple behavioral change. He was stuck until he decided to believe something more compatible with being one of the guys. Being willing was still a SpeedBump for Eldon, but he wasn't quite as *blind* as he'd been before.

Caution: Don't read this chapter and assume we're saying there is anything Eldon *has* to do. It's not a question of whether thoughts and behaviors are right or wrong as much as whether they produce the results you want. Eldon decided he wanted to be considered one of the guys. Until he modifies the very thing that drives his behavior to act superior, Eldon will not transform his BlindSpot in the way he wants. He won't be one of the guys. And until he sees that his willingness is only on the surface of the BlindSpot, he'll just keep asking the same questions, getting the same answer, trying to alter behavior which will be sabotaged by his old pattern of beliefs – a classic BlindSpot.

SpotCheck™:

Be really willing to consider change below the surface of the BlindSpot.

Be willing to see when any of your beliefs or behaviors are in conflict with one another.

Be willing to recognize when you see only two polar options.

As we said, when you hear yourself claiming that you are completely willing to change . . . not so fast.

CHAPTER FIFTEEN

Good Intention, Bad Result

After spotting a BlindSpot, clarify your own Intentions and the Impact which other people are experiencing.

Anita's story:

One day Anita went shopping in a shoe store. They were having some kind of anniversary sale, giving away balloons, and handing out little hot dogs and soft drinks. Anita sat down to try on some shoes.

As she was waiting for the sales person to bring out her shoes, a young man with a big tray of soft drinks approached. She saw his nametag said "Warren." As Warren was asking, "Would you care for something to drink?" he tripped on a discarded shoe box and, as he was falling, dumped the entire tray of soft drinks right on Anita. She was drenched – and sticky.

In her shock, Anita jumped up yelling, "You drowned me!" The embarrassed young man jumped up, said, "I'll be right back," and ran to the back room. In seconds he was back with a big towel and proceeded to mop up the carpet, completely ignoring Anita. Anita could feel the soda running down her legs and realized she was soaked to the skin. She admitted later that she shrieked, but also claimed she had every right to do so. Grabbing Warren by the arm as he rigorously scrubbed the damp carpet, she yelled, "What about me? I'm soaked to the skin. Get me a towel. What is wrong with you?"

Warren stood up and to everyone's amazement, shouted back, "Don't yell at me lady, I didn't do it on purpose."

Provoked further by this response, Anita continued to shriek, "Nobody said you did it on purpose. Get me a towel. You drenched me with soda."

"I didn't mean to. I was being very careful," said Warren.

"Will you get me a towel and leave that stupid carpet alone. I am the customer you know! And now I'm soaked and freezing too, you baboon!" Anita growled, obviously at the end of her rope.

Moving menacingly in Anita's direction, the young man matched her growl and snarled, "Lady, stop making such a scene. I didn't mean to spill drinks on you. I told you, I was being very careful. You're acting like I did the whole thing on purpose."

Mercifully, a manager arrived with a towel for Anita and apologized profusely. He sent Warren up to a register and continued apologizing.

Finally dried off and placated, Anita told the manager she was going home to change. The manager invited her to come back and ask for him personally so he could be sure she got the kind of treatment that would make her feel like a valued customer.

> As the manager escorted Anita out of the store, she passed the register and couldn't resist glaring one more time at Warren. Warren, nothing if not consistent, mumbled under his breath, "I didn't mean to." The manager hustled a sputtering Anita out the door and was seen apologizing outside for quite awhile.

We find the issues of Intention-Impact™ thoroughly illustrated in customer service situations every day. If you have any trouble understanding the concepts we're about to discuss, just pay attention the next time an unhappy customer is trying to get satisfaction. Whether or not the complaint is handled effectively, you'll see a perfect Intention-Impact lesson.

In every interaction, there are always two parts of the exchange – two parts in both directions.

For each person, there are Intentions – what you hope to accomplish by the way you engage others, what you say, and how you express yourself. There are usually SurfaceIntentions™, the reasons you *think* you're expressing yourself in a particular way, and DeepIntentions™, the reasons closer to survival issues that generate how you're expressing yourself. The DeepIntentions may be unconscious and completely hidden, so they are a great place for BlindSpots to lurk. SurfaceIntentions may be entirely true, but seldom encompass the whole picture.

The other part of any exchange is the Impact – how the other person experiences the interaction. Like

Intentions, people usually experience Impact on both a surface level and a deep level. Most people can quickly and easily articulate the SurfaceImpact™. The DeepImpact™ is often hidden or invisible to the person experiencing it. More lurking BlindSpots.

If you think all this Intention-Impact business makes interacting with other people complicated, you're entirely correct. When your Intention matches another person's Impact, you've had a successful exchange. When it doesn't match, you have not been successful, and if something isn't changed, a perfectly innocent exchange can turn into a disaster.

Symptom: You think you've spotted a BlindSpot.
SpotDoctorsRx:
Examine your Intentions and the Impact they are having on others. There are lots of issues in a BlindSpot and what trapped Anita and Warren in open warfare were Intention-Impact issues. Select some exchanges where it might show up and look at both sides.

Intention: What do you want or hope to have happen on the other side of a specific exchange?

Impact: What is actually happening on the other side of this specific exchange as experienced by the other person?

Can you hear Spot barking?

WoofWoof: If you think your motives are often misunderstood, dig deeper.

When you think about Warren's contribution to the soda-dousing episode, you can see he was completely stuck in his Intentions. The real Impact was almost invisible to him.

We'll assume that Warren's SurfaceIntention, because he kept stating it over and over, was to be careful.

Unfortunately, with all his dedication to being careful, he still doused Anita with soda. His Intention did not match his Impact. He had not been successful. And all the assertion of his Intention did nothing to undo the dousing. Focusing only on half of the exchange – Intention – prevented Warren from responding in a way that might reduce the negative Impact. He didn't do anything to help Anita recover or get dry. His Intention to be careful had him *carefully* scrubbing the stained carpet and ignoring Anita's condition.

Because he knew he hadn't doused Anita on purpose – and he focused only on that half of the exchange – his only response seemed to be to claim his innocence. And he continued to be frustrated by the fact that Anita continued to ignore his expressed Intention.

The fact that she was dripping soda the whole time she was complaining was completely lost on Warren.

Can you hear Spot barking?

WoofWoof: Good Intentions do not remove a bad Impact.

To diagnose a BlindSpot, we don't have to examine Warren's DeepIntentions to explain why his strategy accelerated an already difficult situation. But if we looked for deeper Intentions, we'd probably find Warren was doing everything he could to make sure he wasn't blamed for the accident and didn't look bad to his manager. Clearly, Warren's behavior ensured he would get precisely what we're guessing he didn't want – to be blamed and look bad to his manager.

This is a classic BlindSpot – you get exactly what your behavior was designed to avoid.

If Warren had factored in Impact at any point during his encounter with Anita, it would have been immediately apparent to him that no matter how careful he'd meant to be, he still doused an innocent customer. His Impact wasn't perceived as "careful." Had he ever factored in Impact, he would have noticed that it was the doused customer who needed attention if he were to achieve his desired SurfaceIntentions and DeepIntentions.

If Warren had been able to detect what we suspect were his DeepIntentions – self-preservation with his boss – he would have realized how what he was doing would look disastrous.

It takes some practice to be able to find DeepIntentions. But don't worry. SurfaceIntentions can keep you occupied for quite awhile if you continue to ignore the Impact you're having.

Anita doesn't get off the hook in this Intention-Impact lesson, although we'll confess that our natural sympathy is with the wet customer. However, when you examine Anita's SurfaceIntentions, they were probably just to get someone to notice she had been doused and then get her a towel so she could clean up. It seems perfectly sensible. Notice that her strategy for that Intention didn't work. The more she shrieked, the more Warren resisted everything but bellowing his innocence in response. She never did get a towel from him, no matter how much she shrieked – or dripped.

If Anita had noticed she wasn't creating the Impact she wanted and if she had done anything other than more of the same, she might have gotten a better response from Warren. She could have said, "I'm absolutely sure you didn't mean to drench me, Warren. But I am wet. Could I borrow your towel?" Warren probably would have given her the towel he was using to wipe the carpet, and might even have gone for a dry one. We're sure someone who was watching the scene would have nominated Anita for sainthood if she could have produced that level of response, but it might have gotten her what she needed and wanted.

We're not suggesting that responding with attention to Intention **and** Impact is the easiest thing to do. We are suggesting it is much more likely to create what you want.

We're also suggesting you'd be a highly savvy communicator if you could think quickly enough to acknowledge another person's Intention with soda running down your legs. It's a definite distraction. And that's why new response patterns need to be practiced until they are always available, even in a crisis.

Symptom: You think you've spotted a BlindSpot.

SpotDoctorsRx:

Look for situations where you might be noticing and responding to only one part of the interaction.

Practice identifying your own Intentions – both surface and deep.

Practice acknowledging to yourself the full Impact you observe.

Practice acknowledging to yourself the Impact you hear described by others but can't understand.

To help ConnectTheDots with this Rx, put yourself in the driver's seat of a car backing out of your friend's driveway. As you're trying to avoid the flowers, you accidentally run over your friend's foot. He screams and you jump out yelling, "I didn't mean to!"

Your Intention was to be careful about your friend's flowers. Certainly your DeepIntention was to maintain both the friendship and your friend's safety. You avoided the flowers – success. You injured your friend – Impact. You didn't mean to – Intention. Your friend's feet are hurt – Impact.

Applying the SpotDoctorsRx:
Practice identifying your own Intentions – both surface and deep.

You know your SurfaceIntention was to be careful with the flowers. It should be easy to remind yourself of your DeepIntentions regarding the relationship.

Applying the SpotDoctorsRx:
Practice acknowledging to yourself the full Impact you observe.

In this example, you easily notice that you've avoided the flowers – partial Impact. However, your response suggests you aren't really acknowledging your friend's smashed foot – missed Impact. Your "I didn't mean to," focuses only on Intention.

Applying the SpotDoctorsRx:
Practice acknowledging to yourself the Impact you hear described, but don't understand.

The screaming of your friend describes the Impact of your side trip over his foot. This loud expression will help direct you to the Impact which needs to be acknowledged – to yourself, and certainly to your injured friend.

CHAPTER SIXTEEN

It Makes No Sense to Me . . .

It's easy to be seduced by your good Intentions. You can get blind-sided when you assume or act as though your Intention *should* produce the Impact you want. Holding on to your good Intentions to justify your behavior will get you stuck. Good Intentions alone are not enough to ensure effective communication or interaction. Your willingness to adjust your response gives you options to create the intended Impact. If the Impact itself or how the Impact is described by others makes no sense to you, you will stay stuck.

If you can't understand another person's position, concerns, or issues it will be difficult to understand and respond to the whole issue of Intention-Impact.

> You can probably sympathize when someone is troubled by something that would also trouble you.

> You can probably empathize when someone is hurt by something that would hurt you.

> You can probably understand when someone

is upset or reactive about something that would upset or activate you.

When you sympathize, empathize, and understand, it's pretty easy to notice the Impact a person is experiencing – especially if you're not involved.

However, if you can't sympathize, empathize, or understand – and especially if you're involved in the interaction – you may not be as aware, as clever, as flexible, or as positively responsive as you are capable of being. You're more likely to get hooked by a BlindSpot when you're involved inside the situation – where blame, defense, and justification travel with Spot.

SpotCheck™:

> Notice how you react to other people's expression of Impact, whether you understand their perspective or not.

> Notice your reaction and response to the other person.

Your inability to express sympathy, empathy, or understanding – especially when things don't make sense – may prevent you from truly unmasking your BlindSpot.

Mr. First Class's story:

> The plane had just pulled up to the gate, the doors opened, and from the jetway everyone in the gate area could hear a commotion. A man's voice was getting louder and louder as he

approached the crowd waiting to board. "I got nothing. I got a stupid menu and no food. I'm in first class and I got nothing to eat the whole flight!" Mr. First Class was heard shouting as he popped through the door. He waved an airline menu in his hand and railed.

As he stomped around the line and up to the ticket agent, he continued to rant and rave about not getting any food on his flight. He kept spitting out the words, "I got – nothing – nothing," and ripped his airplane menu into little pieces. He threw the pieces on the desk in front of the ticket agent, again screaming he got "nothing" to eat on the plane.

As frequent flyers we have to ask why anyone would ever be upset about not getting airline food. It was a perfect opportunity for us to check our ability to express sympathy or understanding for something that didn't naturally make any sense. Again, enough about us. Right now, we have a rabid Mr. First Class and a ticket agent with a shredded menu in front of her. We were interested in how much compassion she would be able to generate to handle what was obviously a negative Impact on Mr. First Class.

As Mr. First Class continued to vent, the ticket agent, without ever making eye contact with this irate customer, began to patiently put the pieces of the menu back together. She continued to reassemble the menu as Mr. First Class turned on his heel and stomped down the concourse, grumbling loudly enough for everyone to hear again that he "got nothing."

With the coast clear, the ticket agent looked up, rolled her eyes, shook her head, and exchanged glances with most of the passengers in line which clearly implied, "What a psycho!"

Mr. First Class's upset over being handed a menu, but no food, was never addressed. Nobody offered sympathy, empathy, or understanding for the Impact this had on him – no matter how absurd or unexplainable the upset was to anyone else. You can bet that someone eventually had to endure his upset as it continued to fester. And heaven help the next flight attendant who has to tell him there's still no food and he "gets nothing."

There will be those of you reading this chapter who immediately relate to Mr. First Class. You can see why he was so upset. It may even remind you of the time they ran out of peanuts on your flight. You were quite put out. And if you can relate, if it makes sense to you, notice the need to address the Impact is crystal clear. You'd know exactly what to do or say to Mr. First Class. Because it would come naturally, you could offer sympathy for – or at least understanding of – the Impact. A simple, "Oh no, you got nothing?" might have worked wonders.

There will be those of you reading this chapter who are thinking, "Get a life . . . it's airline food for crying out loud." You will, from that perspective, understand the ticket agent's failure to deal with the customer's upset. After all, you think this guy was a psycho too.

Most people reading this chapter may not understand why the ticket agent chose to put the menu back together. We don't know either, and it remains one of the most interesting responses we've ever observed.

When you automatically understand the Impact and relate to the person's feelings, it is easier to address the other person's concerns and account for the Impact. When someone is reacting in a way that makes no sense to you or reacting with feelings which make no sense to you, it is a much greater challenge to attend to Impact. It is therefore easier to dismiss the Impact, because in your mind it is nonsense.

Can you hear Spot barking?

WoofWoof: Your response to someone's stated Impact can make it better or worse.

Symptom: You think you spotted a BlindSpot.
SpotDoctorsRx:
Examine your sympathy, empathy, and understanding CompassionPatterns™.

Note the times you relate to the Impact someone else is experiencing and note also the times you are unable to relate. Start looking at the people you routinely think make no sense and you'll probably find you don't attend to the Impact part of your interaction with them often – or at all.

Notice your own reactions and feelings when someone fails to acknowledge the Impact you're experiencing.

This is not to say that you have to attend to all Impact, everywhere, all the time. It is a choice. The question is, can you attend to Impact when you want? Even the most naturally compassionate people have trouble attending to Impact when it doesn't make sense to them. Learn to recognize and acknowledge your reaction patterns and the limitations that follow. When other people's description or demonstration of Impact seems so off the wall, so trite, so ridiculous . . . so unlike you – can you find a more understanding way to respond?

CHAPTER SEVENTEEN

What Cost?

Many people think of "cost" only in terms of money. That is certainly one way to assess cost and in our culture, usually a pretty motivating one. If you realize your automatic patterns are costing you big bucks, you might be more creative in how to change your patterns.

There are other costs to consider besides money. If you find there is no dollar amount attached to your BlindSpot, look at other values that are important to you. Are healthy relationships important to you? Are you troubled when you haven't behaved responsibly? Is it a concern that people don't appreciate you for who you think you are? Is stress a problem?

These are just a few ways a BlindSpot can carry an enormous price tag. If you think what you are doing is not worth changing, you will not change. It is that simple. You can't fully evaluate the worth of change unless you take the time to examine the cost of your unchanged behavior to yourself and others. Your inability to Spot cost could be one of your most troublesome BlindSpots. You do not want things to deteriorate because you don't realize the cost until it is too late.

Can you hear Spot barking?

WoofWoof: "How much does it cost?" is a question you are willing to ask about virtually anything but the Impact of your behavior.

Phoebe's story:

Clarise had a favorite restaurant for quiet Sunday breakfasts with her husband. It was called Gonzo's Soup Kitchen and Clarise knew Gonzo personally. She always had wonderful service, wonderful food, and a wonderful time with her husband.

Gonzo sold the restaurant, but Clarise and her husband continued to go there, even though they noticed little changes they didn't like. One day they noticed a big change they really didn't like.

Clarise loved the Gonzo Special. It was an omelet full of red bell peppers, cheese, onions, and bacon. She couldn't remember a time at Gonzo's when she'd ordered anything else. But Clarise liked her bacon cooked really well, so she'd learned to always order it "very well done." She'd given up on ordering it "crispy" when it came out amazingly crispy – but amazingly raw – so many times before.

One Sunday Clarise ordered her Gonzo

Special – with the bacon cooked very well done. To her disappointment, the Gonzo Special arrived with almost raw bacon on it. Clarise called the waitress back and said, "This bacon is raw." The waitress snipped, "You can't get it crispy in the Gonzo Special." She walked away before Clarise could even respond.

The busboy came by to pour coffee, asked how everything was, and when Clarise said her bacon was raw, he smiled and said, "Fine," and walked away.

Clarise gave up, moved the disgusting raw bacon aside and finished her meal. The waitress came with the check, never again speaking to Clarise or her husband.

When Clarise's husband paid the bill, the new owner, Phoebe, was behind the register. She was a sour person, and looked particularly sour that day. As Clarise stood by her husband, she heard Phoebe ask, "So how was everything?" Clarise immediately said, "My bacon on the Gonzo Special was raw." Phoebe, still looking at Clarise's husband, gave what apparently was the restaurant party line saying, "You can't get the bacon crispy in the Gonzo Special."

A little tired of hearing this lame excuse, Clarise leaned forward and said measuredly, "I didn't ask for it crisp. I asked for it well done."

"Same thing," growled Phoebe, finally making eye contact.

"No, it is not the same thing," said Clarise through slightly clenched teeth. "Well done means cooked. I don't care how floppy or limber or soft the bacon is, I just want it cooked."

"Well, you should have explained that to your waitress," said the intractable Phoebe.

"I thought saying well done was explanation enough," snapped Clarise. "And when I told her it was raw, she did nothing. And the busboy did nothing, and now you're doing nothing. No one has even said they were sorry my bacon was raw," said Clarise in a voice squeaking with her frustration and effort to control her temper.

Phoebe looked Clarise dead in the eye and said, "The reason no one has said they are sorry about your bacon is because we're NOT sorry."

Clarise was so taken aback she could only sputter for a minute. Finally she got the words out, "Do you care about any future business with us?"

"Nope," said Phoebe.

"Do you care about your reputation for customer service?" asked Clarise, believing more and more that she was stuck in a Twilight Zone episode.

"Nope," said Phoebe.

"Do you think you can stay in business treating people this way?"

"Yep," said the *Gary Cooper* of Gonzo's Soup Kitchen.

Clearly Phoebe is a person incapable of assessing the cost of her actions. Who in their right mind would expect to maintain a business by treating customers this way? Who in their right mind would return to a business like this after being told no one was sorry about their treatment?

On one level, Phoebe's Intention and the Impact her behavior is having are completely congruent. Phoebe wants Clarise to know that no one is sorry and

Clarise clearly knows that. If only communication were so simple and one-dimensional.

We're guessing that Phoebe, unless she was completely self-destructive, also had an Intention to succeed in business. The Impact Phoebe had on her customer was unlikely to result in that Impact. So the cost of one pattern of behavior, although congruent and highly successful in one way, generated costs Phoebe surely did not want to pay. Too bad for Phoebe she couldn't ConnectTheDots.

Symptom: You think you've spotted a BlindSpot.

SpotDoctorsRx:

Look at your BlindSpot **3**Dimensionally™. To look at the BlindSpot in only a linear fashion may be misleading.

Factor in extended costs in as many directions as you can. When you see the **3**Dimensional BlindSpot for what it is, a variety of changes will be available.

Your BlindSpots can cost you relationships, health, success, happiness, and your future. As long as you don't recognize the costs, you will be unlikely to choose to alter your patterns in any constructive way. Why would you?

Phoebe didn't. Don't be a Phoebe.

CHAPTER EIGHTEEN

Have You Been Spinning Your Brains Out?

Ronald Reagan's Story:

When Ronald Reagan was running for President of the United States, he realized that Walter Mondale was going to make an issue out of his age. So in their first televised debates, Reagan announced that he understood that age was a consideration in the election and pledged that he wouldn't use Mr. Mondale's youth and inexperience against him. He brought down the house. There are many political and media commentators who believe Reagan won the election that night.

Most people are familiar with political spin. The political arena even invented the term "spin doctors" for the people who turn something potentially bad into something potentially good – or at least no longer bad. What most people don't know is that we're all spin doctors. We're spinning all the time.

We seriously doubt that people can stop spinning completely or would even want to if they could. We believe people can do better in recognizing that they do Spin, when they are Spinning, and when the Spin is getting them into trouble – BlindSpots trouble.

Symptom: You think you've Spotted a BlindSpot.

SpotDoctorsRx:

Learn that Spin is Fiction. It's a story or interpretation you make up to explain or enhance some Fact that you observe.

Fact is observable.

Fact is seldom debatable.

If you look at a thermometer on your office wall and it registers 70 degrees, most people will agree that the temperature reads 70 degrees. One step beyond this factual observation lie all kinds of Fiction – Spin. Someone declares that the office is hot. Someone else says, "Are you crazy? It's freezing in here." The Spin debate has begun.

You may have heard the story of the three umpires who were asked, "How do you know when a pitch is a strike?" The first novice umpire answered, "I call them as I see them." The second novice umpire replied, "I call them as they are." The third, experienced umpire smiled and responded, "They ain't nothing 'til I call 'em."

The experienced umpire understood the pitch going over the plate had no meaning until he gave it meaning. Likewise, events you experience only get meaning from you. You make the mistake of thinking the Fact is the same as your Fiction.

Fact: The pitch went somewhere over the plate. This event is observable and undeniable and can be verified with instant replay.

Fiction: The pitch is a strike. This is Fiction – in many cases, highly debatable fiction. Go to a baseball game and you will observe countless fans acting on their Fiction as Fact.

Fiction is often treated as Fact in your life. An event happens and you make the call – an interpretation. Your life experiences, beliefs, and values all influence how you interpret the event. But it is still just an interpretation – a Spin.

Observe the workings of a courtroom. The attorneys for the prosecution and defense operate with the same observable Facts. There is blood at the crime scene. There is a weapon. There are fingerprints, DNA, and physical evidence – Facts. The interpretation of those facts is where the attorneys differ. The ultimate goal of both the prosecution and the defense is to convince twelve jurors that their Spin is Fact.

BlindSpots feed on Spin.

Symptom: You think you've spotted a BlindSpot.
SpotDoctorsRx:
Learn the rules of Spin.

SpinRules™:

Your assertions are usually Fiction – Spin, no matter how much they feel like Fact to you.

Your Spin is your automatic leap from something observed to the story you make up about it – what you decide it means.

Your Spin appears to be correct often enough to keep you Spinning confidently.

Your Spin is designed to assist you in guessing and predicting to facilitate quick decisions. Quick doesn't necessarily mean accurate.

Spinning and receiving Spin can be equally hazardous.

Spin can be used to justify, defend, and lock you into your righteous position.

Spin can be used to explain your less-than-constructive responses.

Spin creates a lens that further distorts any subsequent Fact.

Spinning is so automatic, you may have trouble figuring out what you observed which prompted the Spin in the first place.

Burt's Story:

Burt worked with John, the Vice President of a very large corporation. Burt hadn't been with the company long, but long enough to realize that John was an important player. From the first moment Burt met John he was put off. For no reason he could articulate, he thought John was arrogant and distant. It made him uncomfortable and ill at ease whenever John was around.

It wasn't long before Burt's discomfort began to show in his behavior. He sometimes found himself babbling almost incoherently in John's presence. When he was around John, his memory was so bad John once asked him if he was feeling ok. The more anxiety Burt felt, the more his confidence slipped and the more he was sure John was out to get him.

One day he received a memo from John saying that he'd assigned Burt a mentor, Helen, and that they were scheduled for lunch that same day. Burt was sure this was the beginning of the end.

At lunch, he found Helen to be personable,

professional, and seemingly helpful. She assured him that their relationship was strictly confidential, "Unless you tell me you're planning a crime," she joked. Burt found himself smiling in spite of his Spin-inspired paranoia. After several meetings he found himself trusting Helen and accepting her counsel.

When Burt finally admitted to Helen that he thought John didn't like him and that he also thought John was arrogant, Helen was surprised. She'd known John for years and had never thought of him as arrogant. But she was curious about what gave Burt this impression.

At first Burt couldn't say what had made him think John was arrogant or why he disliked him. With patient queries, Helen helped John discover that his whole Spin about John had started with what Burt described as "that look." With more gentle probing from Helen, Burt finally described John as "always looking down his nose at everyone."

Helen broke into a big smile and said, "I understand completely. Burt, this is going to be so easy. And thank you for reminding me again of what all of us who've been with the company so long take completely for granted."

Burt was intrigued and asked, "What do you mean?"

"Well," said Helen, still smiling, "I can easily see where you might have interpreted John's behavior as arrogant or looking down on you. That's exactly what he's doing."

"What?" gasped John, horrified to hear that his worst fears were being confirmed.

"No, no," Helen said, seeing where he was going. "I only meant that he tilts his head up and looks down on everyone. He has some strange thing with his focus and can't really see head on. He has to lift up his chin to focus. And then he wears those awful little Ben Franklin glasses on the end of his nose. No wonder you thought what you thought. You see, most of us knew John long before he had his eye condition. And we were here while he was figuring out how to hold his head so he could see. We don't even notice any more."

"Are you kidding me about this?" Burt asked, still skeptical.

"Of course not. And I want to thank you for bringing this to my attention. I want to speak to John about it, without mentioning you. It is something he needs to be aware of when he interacts with new people."

"Are you sure he's going to appreciate your speaking to him about something so personal?" asked Burt, still clinging to his original Spin on John.

"Oh, he's used to it, Burt. I was his mentor once, too," said Helen, giving Burt a smile and a wonderful imitation of John's head tilt.

All Burt had seen was a particular way John held his head but he proceeded to Spin a whole story about who John was and how he felt about Burt. Once the initial Spin was in place, anything John did that would lend itself to Burt's interpretation was seen as more evidence that Burt was right about John.

Can you hear Spot barking?

WoofWoof: The initial Spin sets up a perceptual lens that creates a self-fulfilling prophecy.

Burt had been sure that his Fiction – Spin – was Fact. And his SpunFact had created so much anxiety in him that he sabotaged his own confidence and performance in John's presence.

The one piece of good news about Spin is that it works the other way too. If you Spin a constructive Fiction, it may actually impact your behavior in a positive way. If you think people like you, value your contribution, and appreciate your competence, you can see where it could bring out the best in you.

Whether the Spin is working constructively or destructively, knowing that you Spin and getting good at separating Fact from Fiction is a highly productive skill.

Symptom: You think you've spotted a BlindSpot.
SpotDoctorsRx:
Practice separating Fact from Fiction.

Unravel any Spin that might be getting you off course and feeding your BlindSpot.

Sometimes a BlindSpot is simply your habitual way of Spinning in a particular direction. That's really handy to know. Once you know the direction, you can then decide how to Spin in a more constructive way.

Because – Spin you will. It might be in human DNA.

CHAPTER NINETEEN

More About Spin

Remember David from Chapter Eight? He was the guy who thought the people in the classroom were about to be wished a "Happy Birthday."

Another David story:

David lives in a lovely area of the southwest where the sun shines almost every day and he can spend time in his hot tub every night. One night he was relaxing in the hot tub gazing at the stars.

He heard lots of whooping and yelling in the distance. He smiled. "Wow, someone's having quite a party," he thought to himself. The next night, as he again relaxed in the hot tub at the end of the day, he heard the same group apparently in heavy revelry again. After several nights of experiencing the same thing, David was convinced that his distant neighbors were true party animals.

Some weeks later, in idle conversation with his next-door neighbor Harold, David asked if he knew who was always having the wild parties. Harold looked perplexed and asked, "What wild parties? What are you talking about?" Harold's wife walked up just as David was saying, "The people who live over there, the ones you can hear every night yelling and having such a good time." Harold and his wife couldn't stifle their guffaws. Barely able to get their breath, they both squeaked, "You mean the coyotes?"

David seems to Spin in a somewhat predictable way. We wouldn't generalize with just two stories, so understand that we've had plenty of experience watching him Spin a party out of almost anything. David walks around with a party lens ready and waiting.

We know it hadn't been a troublesome pattern for David yet – until the Begonia episode.

David and the Begonias:

David and his wife were driving to visit their lifelong friends. As they approached Treenie and Lisa's house, David saw them standing in the yard anticipating his visit.

"Look at them," he said, "they're outside to greet us. Bet they've planned something special."

As David approached the driveway, Treenie bolted toward the van, waving and yelling. Lisa was jumping up and down.

"They are so glad to see us," said David. "I've never seen them this excited." David parked the car and jumped out ready to receive hugs all around.

"My Begonias!" Treenie screamed as he got to the van.

"What?" said David, very puzzled by this particular endearment.

"My Begonias, my Begonias, you drove over my Begonias. We were trying to signal you, but you wiped them out." David was clueless. He never noticed the Begonias, only the perceived excitement he saw in his friends' actions.

David's automatic Spin had made it impossible to consider that his friends were signaling anything wrong or bad. It's only Begonias this time, but at some point, it could mean bigger trouble for David. We're just guessing, but without the flexibility of interpretation that comes with Spin awareness, David just might see an angry mob as an approaching party. That could be a problem. An angry mob can wipe out anyone's Begonias.

Remember Myrtle from Chapter One, who was stuck being up at midnight because her bed was already made?

Another Myrtle Story:

Myrtle came home from her volunteer work one day very upset. One of her earrings was missing. She was saying to her son Bob, "They stole my earring. I know it." Bob, trying to make sense, said, "You think someone took one earring right off your ear? Mom, that doesn't make any sense. Maybe you dropped it."

"I did not drop it," said Myrtle. "You are just so trusting, you don't think anyone would steal anything."

"I don't think anyone is stupid enough to steal one earring, Mom. What is someone going to do with one earring?" Bob asked.

Later that afternoon, Bob walked in the house with the missing earring. "Where did you find that? Did someone bring it back?" demanded Myrtle when she saw the earring. "It was in the driveway, Mom, very close to where you dropped the last one," said Bob.

Myrtle appears to have a Spin pattern magnetized toward mistrusting others. We have observed her on many occasions, misplacing something, asserting that it was stolen, only to find it somewhere in her bedroom – where the bed is always made.

Myrtle, one more time:

One day Myrtle was in her bedroom laying out money on her well-made bed. She was giving her eight nieces and nephews money for the holidays and wanted to be sure she had the right number of $5 bills and envelopes.

Bob stuck his head around the corner and said, "Mom, dinner is ready." Myrtle threw herself across the bed, covering up the $5 bills that were lying there.

"What are you doing?" asked her son. "Nothing," said Myrtle. Bob was used to his mother's paranoid behavior, but felt he had to ask, "Mom, do you think I'm going to steal your money?" Myrtle said an emphatic, "No!" but continued to lie on the money. "Well come on to dinner then," Bob said. It was only after he'd left the room and heard the door lock on the other side that he was sure his mother had left the bed.

We know Bob and can tell you with complete confidence that he doesn't steal from his mother. If you asked his mother, she'd say the same thing. She'd be puzzled about why you would ever think such a thing. None of these facts, however, kept Myrtle from her habitual Spin. She flung herself across her money as though the Crime of the Century were about to be committed in her room.

This Spin pattern could go on for years completely out of Myrtle's awareness. And she'd be upset to learn that her son feels she doesn't trust him. But she would have no clue that her behaviors were the result of a Spin pattern – an indiscriminate pattern of interpretation which, regardless of circumstances or people involved, Spins the same direction.

Symptom: You think you've spotted a BlindSpot.
SpotDoctorsRx:
We suspect that everyone has Spin patterns. Investigate yours.

Pay attention to how your Spin impacts your communication.

Be aware of the way your Spin creates miscommunication and mis-understanding – yours and theirs!

Alter your Spin and it will have a direct impact on your experiences and decisions.

This has to be a conscious choice. If you don't choose to change your Spin, you are stuck with the Automatic Spin already in place – a wonderful breeding ground for BlindSpots.

CHAPTER TWENTY

Blah, Blah, Blah

Andy's Story:

Gail mentioned to her friend, Andy, she was going to take her dog to obedience school. Andy immediately said, "Oh, I remember my dog Skippy. I had my first apartment and Skippy turned out to be a chewer. And Skippy blah, blah, blah. And I blah, blah, blah. And doggie school was blah, blah, blah.

After Andy's non-stop diatribe about his experience, Gail, with glazed eyes, wandered off. Andy was completely oblivious to his Impact on Gail or her glazed eyeballs.

Many people believe they are good listeners. We've often heard Andy claim to be a good listener. We've also seen Andy repeat this pattern of shifting all conversations to himself and his experience over and over. It's definitely a recurring pattern.

Most people we've asked claim to know very few, if any, good listeners. Something is wrong here. If many people believe they are good listeners, but claim to know very few – why aren't these people getting together?

More About Andy:

> It wasn't long before Andy's BlindSpot began to catch up with him. Several of his closest friends had, apparently, had enough. They told Andy that he never listened, that he always talked about himself, and that he repeated stories, even when they told him they'd already heard them before.
>
> Andy was shocked. He was positive he was a good listener. He couldn't believe his friends didn't think he listened or responded attentively. And he was very sure he didn't repeat himself.
>
> Andy became quite concerned about his friends' revelations. Given their description of his behavior and his complete lack of recollection regarding any of their accusations, he decided he must have Alzheimer's disease. It was impossible for him to believe he wasn't listening to what other people were saying or that he was so unconsciously redundant.
>
> So Andy went to see the doctor. After a battery of tests, the doctor told Andy, "No Alzheimer's. Actually, Andy, I think your only problem is that you're not a good listener. Apparently you don't even listen to yourself. You've repeated several stories to me just today."

It's hard to imagine that someone would rather believe they have Alzheimer's than consider their listening and responding habits – but that's Andy's BlindSpot. And while not as extreme as Andy, we've seen many people who will label their bad listening, repetition, and self-focus anything but what it is – a momentary and exclusive MeFocus™.

Some people focus on "me" some of the time. Others do almost nothing else. Some people can give others an experience of being attended to completely. Others can't, even when they are really listening. No matter how you rate your listening or focus skills, how well you really listen and how much of your interaction begins and ends with attention only to yourself can provide some helpful BlindSpot direction.

Symptom: You think you've spotted a BlindSpot.
SpotDoctorsRx:
Stop and ask yourself if you really hear and attend to others.

The way you listen and hear other people has a direct impact on your communication and interaction. Engage people in conversations and see if you can be curious – even if the subject isn't about you or it doesn't really interest you. This can be harder than you think and you may uncover a BlindSpot in the process.

Ask for feedback about your listening ability. See if you can be curious while receiving this feedback. If you receive feedback which surprises or concerns you, monitor your future interactions and see if you can identify any automatic listening patterns which are not working.

If you are not listening receptively, you may be missing vital information that could help you uncover your BlindSpots. What you hear others say may give you ideas about how to change your patterns or what Impact your patterns are having. Your ability to let others feel heard can open interaction in all kinds of beneficial directions – for you and for them.

If your focus consistently flips back to you, you are likely to create a perception that you aren't interested in anything but yourself, don't care about how other people feel or what they think, and eventually, someone will want to slap you silly.

Ralph's story:

Ralph and Heather were on a plane returning home from a business trip. Ralph talked incessantly throughout the entire flight. He talked about how well he was doing, how great his sales were going, and how he was sure he was getting a promotion. Heather did nothing to sustain the conversation since Ralph was only too happy to talk about himself. She dozed off a couple of times, awakening to find Ralph still babbling – oblivious to his sleeping audience.

By the time the plane landed, Heather thought her head was going to explode. She had never been so happy to see a trip come to an end. As they walked off the plane, Ralph was still droning on and on about how fantastic he was.

Through blank eyes, Heather spotted her boyfriend Matt in the crowd of greeters. He ran to her with flowers and balloons. Before Heather knew what was happening, Matt was on one knee, kissing her hand and proposing. As Heather's eyes filled with tears, she was horrified to hear Ralph's voice right behind her.

Clueless about the romantic event unfolding right before his eyes, he continued to talk about himself. Heather, at the end of her rope, wanted to slap him silly. What should have been a romantic and private moment for Matt and Heather had morphed into an awkward chatty threesome.

Heather tried to ignore Ralph's presence and said, "Yes!" Unstoppable to the end, Ralph followed them as they raced to baggage claim, gushing details about his own marriage proposal, wedding plans, and honeymoon.

After Matt and Heather had managed to disengage a still yapping Ralph and climb into a taxi, they agreed Ralph was the biggest idiot on the planet. And almost simultaneously said, "And we're not inviting him to the wedding either."

There are so many BlindSpots in this story you'd have to be *blind* yourself not to Spot them. Ralph, on the other hand, had tightened his focus so much on himself, he missed even the most obvious clues. In this instance, he was the uncontested champion of MeFocus.

ExclusionaryBehavior™ – which shuts another person out – is no better or worse than InclusionaryBehavior

– which invites someone in. They are simply the polar extremes of what is available in any interaction. The problem arises when a person, like Ralph, doesn't know or care which kind of behavior is being chosen or utilized. Or worse yet, people may be able to identify the behavior but don't know how to apply that awareness in a flexible or constructive way.

ExclusionaryBehavior is anything that disengages a mutual experience. It is a way of putting people off, pushing them away, shutting them out. There are times and circumstances where this behavior may be quite appropriate. When riding a subway, no one wants to *include* the entire subway car in the experience. It's when inclusion would be the appropriate choice and you don't employ it that a BlindSpot is probably present. If Ralph were engaging in a conversation *with* Heather, she should have been a part of it. She wasn't. It's hard to imagine how Ralph could have made her less a part of the conversation except by pushing her out of the plane.

Of course, if Ralph's Intention was to engage in a conversation only with himself, he was right on target. The seat next to him could have been empty for all he cared. But we'd have to be *MindReaders* to know his Intentions. Heather, like most people, will fill in the blanks, Spin, and attribute Intentions to Ralph (*MindReading*) – whether they are correct or not.

InclusionaryBehavior is anything which makes people part of a mutual experience. It is a way of pulling people in, joining with them, creating a shared experience. When you are engaged with other people, unless you *want* them to feel left out, InclusionaryBehavior is appropriate – even desirable.

A genuine interest in other people is required to generate InclusionaryBehavior automatically.

We don't know whether Ralph actually meant to exclude Heather or he is just clueless to this BlindSpot. No one else will know either without asking Ralph.

Symptom: You think you've spotted a BlindSpot in someone else.
SpotDoctorsRx:
Tactfully ask the other person what their Intentions are and listen with curiosity.

This is just information for you. Caution: You'll want to go further and point out their cluelessness, but remember (please!) this book is not written so that you can bludgeon others about their BlindSpots.

Your interest, curiosity, and InclusionaryBehavior can create a positive, inviting, and constructive experience on the other side of your interactions. If Ralph had wanted to *include* Heather in the conversation, he needed to be interested in what she thought and said. He certainly needed to notice when she was asleep. And later, when Matt was proposing, excluding himself completely would have been a sensitive and compassionate choice for Ralph to make. He didn't make it.

Symptom: You think you've spotted a BlindSpot.

SpotDoctorsRx:

Identify your InclusionaryBehaviors.

Identify your ExclusionaryBehaviors.

Step into other people's shoes and evaluate how much a part of things they may be feeling. (Notice their cues.)

ConnectTheDots between how you imagine they are feeling and your behavior.

Log the number of times you make a dismissal judgment about the person on the other side of your conversation.

Here are some typical Inclusionary and Exclusionary behaviors – both thoughts and actions – to help ConnectTheDots with this Rx.

InclusionaryBehavior
Expressing genuine interest and curiosity about another person.
Having the ability to notice and respond to cues given by another person.
Creating space for others to contribute.
Acknowledging other's contribution.
Building on the other side of the conversation.

Speaking in "we" and "us" terms.

Using open nonverbal behavior – smiling, direct eye contact, head nodding, encouraging gestures, orienting body toward a person.

Employing accepting thoughts, words, and facial expressions.

Limiting your MeFocus.

ExclusionaryBehavior

Holding a deeply held belief that your own experiences are the only ones with any value.

Having an inability to notice or a lack of interest in responding to cues given by another person.

Shifting all topics and circumstances back to you.

Speaking only in "I" terms.

Creating no space for contribution from anyone else.

Failing to acknowledge any contribution on the other side of the conversation.

Using closed nonverbal behavior – sour or no facial expression, orienting body away from a person, "stop" gestures.

Allowing negative judgments about the person or what they are saying which will leak out in words and expression.

Wallowing in MeFocus.

MeFocus – being persistently egocentric – creates a generally negative experience for people on the other side of your interactions. It's hard to Spot because to you, your interactions *feel* so engaged. You may be surprised to hear that we think you are engaged. You are *fully and completely engaged* – but only with yourself. Trust us – this MeFocus engagement is only enjoyable for you. And if that's all you care about, this BlindSpot will trip you up again and again. You'll probably never know until it's too late – how could you?

BlindSpots - Section FOUR

The Roads Not Taken.

We all find ourselves at crossroads every day. And at every crossroad you have an opportunity to make choices, many choices.

We call the problematic opportunities for choices **BlindSpot Crossings™**.

Some are big serious ones and some are so inconsequential you might not realize they are a BS-Xing™ at all.

The choices you make when there are alternative paths to take – and there are usually many paths available – can highlight your ability to be awake, aware, curious, and versatile.

Or it can highlight a BlindSpot.

CHAPTER TWENTY-ONE

Who Gets the Cheese?

People in the service industry experience countless BS-Xings in the course of a day. Their MindSet is challenged with every encounter and their BlindSpots can appear as often as the Blue Plate Special.

Mac's Story:

> Mac took his wife to Red Pepper's Restaurant one day. He loved their nachos and was looking forward to a plate piled high with tostadas and cheese. He always ordered extra cheese.
>
> The waiter delivered the nacho plate with a pitiful amount of cheese on top. He apologized, but explained that the corporate offices were now requiring them to weigh all cheese and he put on as much as he was allowed.
>
> Mac calmly explained he'd be very willing to pay for extra cheese. The waiter said he had no way of charging extra. He simply had to put the required amount of cheese on the nachos and that was all he could do. "Perhaps you'd like to talk to a manager," the waiter said, showing embarrassment over the new

policy and the puny pile of cheese on his customer's plate.

"I certainly would," said Mac. "The nacho plate is a waste of my time without a lot of cheese. It's why I come here."

A few moments later, the manager approached Mac. She was shaking her head "no" and began to explain the corporate policy without even introducing herself.

The cheese debate went back and forth and finally seeing that Mac wasn't giving up, the manager snatched the nacho plate off the table, spat an "Oh, all right!" at Mac, and went into the kitchen.

Several minutes later a new waiter arrived at Mac's table with a nacho plate bathed in cheese – just the way he liked it.

Mac's wife had been silent throughout this whole melodrama. As she watched her husband scarf down the nachos with obvious relish, she said, "Well, I'm glad they could finally satisfy you." To her surprise, Mac slammed his fist down on the table, turned red in the face, and growled at her, "Those asses have no clue about satisfying me!"

"But you got your cheese, dear," said his confused wife.

Mac sputtered, "Don't you get it? I don't care about their precious corporate policy. When I finish this plate and every last ounce of their carefully weighed cheese, we're leaving and we're never coming back!

"But I like Red Pepper's," murmured his wife.

This is an event full of BS-Xings. So many places along the way people had choices they could have made which would have changed at least one person's experience for the better.

The waiter might have explained the policy before bringing out the under-cheesed nachos. Perhaps Mac could have ordered something else that didn't have to be weighed and measured. However, when the waiter saw how much Mac wanted more cheese, he did choose to call in his manager, who had some cheese authority.

The manager barreled through her BS-Xings like a Demolition Derby driver. Before she ever approached the unhappy customer, she had many choices about which MindSet she'd bring with her. Was she going to be helpful, concerned, curious? Apparently she chose to be positional and resistant, communicated clearly by her head-shaking before she'd even made contact with Mac.

The manager faced another BS-Xing when she decided to continue to push the corporate cheese-weighing policy instead of communicating any understanding of Mac's disappointment. She could have stepped into Mac's shoes for a moment, but she chose to remain firmly planted in her own corporate shoes.

Once the manager decided to replace the nachos, she ran over another BS-Xing by snatching the plate away and never returning. Obviously the manager thought that the cheese would be the whole answer. She was very *blind* to the full Impact this episode was having on Mac.

Mac stumbled through several BS-Xings of his own. Instead of growling at his wife, he could have realized how upset he'd allowed himself to become over cheese. We understand his frustration, but without monitoring his Spin or acknowledging his mounting frustration, he was left dumping on his innocent wife.

Mac also had a choice about expressing his upset and frustration to Red Pepper's corporate offices. We're not suggesting this is a necessarily effective solution, but we doubt seriously that anyone at Red Pepper's anywhere noticed that Mac boycotted the restaurant for five years. So Mac's solution did nothing to potentially change the Red Pepper's policy. We have it on good authority that for years Mac relived the "cheese incident," as he called it, every time he drove by Red Pepper's. That's a lot of stress on the nervous system for a little bit of cheese. And, as we said, after five years, Mac finally returned to Red Pepper's, but with a MindSet that never allowed him to be happy there again – no matter how much cheese they gave him.

We're not suggesting that any of these options *should* have been taken. We're simply illustrating that there are often options that *could* be taken which might change the entire direction of an event.

Think of your interactions like a dance. You're out on the floor jitterbugging your brains out. But your partner continues to waltz. You're not a very compatible couple. You may be very amusing to watch, but there is a possibility of serious injury if neither of you changes the dance. And one or both of you will certainly have some reticence about getting on the dance floor together again.

To jitterbug or to waltz is a BS-Xing. Continuing to dance the way you are dancing is a BS stubbornness issue. To tango together is a BS versatility issue. To want to compromise or change the dance is a BS MindSet issue. Thinking your dance partner doesn't care about you is a BS Spin issue. Continuing to build your case about your idiot dance partner is a BS righteousness issue. Noticing any of these issues means you've become a better BlindSpotter. Choosing to do anything new or different about any one of these issues can change the dance – and the experience – and make full use of the BS-Xing to move forward.

If you choose to do nothing different – if you leave the dance floor frustrated, angry, and snarling under your breath about the "idiot" you just danced with – you have walked away from a BS-Xing. From our observations, we want to warn you. This BlindSpot is now on the table – *WoofWoof.* You'll probably dance with an "idiot" again. Welcome to the predictable recurrence of a BS-Xing.

CHAPTER TWENTY-TWO

Am I the Only One Who Cares?

Chevon's story:

On one of her business trips, Chevon was staying at a new hotel. The hotel hadn't been open long and was clearly ironing out the kinks. Everything that could go wrong did go wrong.

The hotel seemed to want to get things right, but they were falling short everywhere. Chevon was an experienced traveler and knew that guest feedback could be helpful.

After a few days of observing multiple snafus, Chevon called the front desk and said, "I'm in room 612 and I have several complaints I'd like to discuss. Please connect me with someone who cares."

She heard a voice mail response on the other end of the line and proceeded to explain her complaints in detail. A few minutes later, Chevon noticed the message light blinking on her phone. She was astounded by the quick response to her complaints and was anxious to hear the voice of the person who had cared so much and been so responsive.

As she listened, she burst into laughter. The operator had connected Chevron to her own voice mail system and she was listening to her own voice explain her complaints. "Well, I guess they connected me to someone who cared – me."

Some of you reading this story probably got upset on Chevon's behalf. What a stupid thing to do – connect her to her own voice mail! You might even have imagined yourself in a similar situation stomping down to the front desk to be sure that the clueless person who connected you to your own voice mail was publicly identified – and punished, if you could pull it off. That's one choice at this BS-Xing.

Chevon, because of her MindSet, her previous patterns, her cultivated patience – who knows – found it funny. Laughter is so good for your nervous system, we recommend it whenever you can create it. And that's the point. Chevon created her response with whatever patterns she's developed to react to frustrating events in a light way.

We're not suggesting that laughter is always the appropriate choice. But you'll notice that when it is an appropriate choice, some people just can't make it.

Harriet's Story:

Harriet asked her husband to help her remove a wall outlet plate. Her husband agreed, but as he was attempting to put one of the screws back, he dropped it into the wall. It disappeared somewhere under the house.

147

Harriet didn't say anything out loud, but rolled her eyes and thought, "I can't believe he just did that." She then ran a little inventory of all the klutzy things her husband had done around the house in the last few months. She sighed, pursed her lips, and walked away – leaving her husband fumbling with the other screw.

Later that evening, Harriet and her husband were watching a sitcom on TV. On the show the husband was spinning his wedding ring and it ended up going down the heater grate.

Harriet was laughing, as she always did at the TV husband's behavior. Her husband stared at her and said, "Why is that funny and the screw falling in the wall wasn't?"

Any wife will probably tell you that a TV husband is funny because he's not *her* husband. But what's going on here is also a MindSet issue. Harriet was ready to laugh at the TV husband, maybe even expected to laugh at him. She carries a MindSet about her husband that doesn't appear to evoke amusement, laughter, even tolerance. While we're sure this MindSet makes it unpleasant for her husband, it also gets Harriet stuck in a rut at each and every BS-Xing. The choice she continues to make yields only big sighs instead of the big laughs available with another MindSet.

You can sigh all you want – and roll your eyeballs – and think someone's an idiot. Or you could choose another path, and laugh like Chevon. It's not a question of what you should do, but what you *could do* and *really want to* do.

At the heart of all BlindSpots improvement is accepting the truth that you've programmed all your beliefs and reactions. You may get some help, but ultimately you are putting your MindSet, your flexibility, your resources, your attitudes into place at every BS-Xing. And you can change all your BS – if you want to.

CHAPTER TWENTY-THREE

Give Yourself Enough Rope

Leonard's story:

Leonard entered his bank one day and noticed the usual velvet ropes zigzagging their way up to the teller desk. He was delighted to see them empty. Indeed, he was the only one in the bank. So he walked up to Bernice's teller window.

As he pushed his deposit toward Bernice, she leaned closer to him and in a conspiratorial whisper said, "Excuse me, sir, but you have to go through the ropes."

"What?" said Leonard, looking around again to be sure the lobby was truly empty. "You're kidding, right?"

"No sir, said Bernice. It's a bank rule. You'll have to walk through the ropes." Leonard began to laugh and look into the upper corners of the bank ceiling. "Am I on Candid Camera or something?" he said, still chuckling.

"No sir," said Bernice sounding rather pitiful, "but if you don't go through the ropes, I'll get in trouble." So Leonard dutifully walked back to the door and meandered first one direction and then the other through the ropes until he arrived back at Bernice's window. She cheerfully accepted his deposit and wished him a good day.

Here's another BS-Xing that could have gone many ways. Leonard obviously has a sense of humor and a heavy dose of patience. His MindSet prompted him to think he was on TV, rather than jumping to a lot of internal conversation about how idiotic the ropes request was. The end result was that he walked out of the bank relaxed and amused, and left Bernice smiling and appreciative.

Leonard's wife's story:

> When Leonard arrived at his car he was still chuckling. His wife, Lola, wanted to know what had happened. As Leonard explained the whole ropes routine, Lola became incensed. "Didn't you ask to speak to a manager?" she yelled. "I would have made one of those pompous bankers explain to me why this rope thing made sense!"
>
> As she said "me" she smacked herself so hard in the chest she coughed. "I can't believe you actually walked through that stupid rope line! Pull around front. I'm going in there. This is ridiculous," continued Lola, scrambling out of her seat belt and clawing for the door handle.

If Lola made it into the bank, you can imagine what happened. We're very sure Bernice, the teller, wouldn't have been smiling when Leonard's wife got through with her. And someone in charge would have had to deal with Lola. And maybe the ropes would have come down or the policy would have been changed. Maybe not. There are all kinds of possibilities on the other side of a BS-Xing.

What we can say with certainty is that Lola's blood pressure shot through the roof, that her heart rate increased, that adrenalin pumped into her system, and she experienced a hundred other chemical and biological changes that accompany stress – all unpleasant and unhealthy for Lola. It's probably not so pleasant or healthy for anyone she runs into while having this stress reaction – the ripple effect of upset.

This was not Lola's first such reaction. She was so instantly good at it that we're sure she's a pro. All this upset and the upset she spewed into the bank probably confirmed all her righteous indignation, and her negative judgments – about both her husband and pompous bankers. The Spin Lola put on the event fired an obvious – but perhaps misapplied – MindSet to stand up for what she thought was right. Imagine, all that from a little velvet rope.

Given the choice Lola was making at this BS-Xing, we're sure she managed to imbed her patterns and reactions even deeper. She never even saw the BS.

Someone send this woman our book!

CHAPTER TWENTY-FOUR

Where's the Loo?

Winston Churchill described Americans and the English as two people separated by a common language. There's more to the "languages" we speak than simple vocabulary. Nuances, inflection, all of the nonverbal elements, and your DeepIntentions make up another aspect of vocabulary. They are seldom thought of as a language or even part of language – a major BlindSpot. The words normally called *vocabulary* are only the tip of the iceberg in terms of people-to-people communication. There are so many ways for people to "speak" and create miscommunication, we've given up counting. However, no matter what the real or symbolic language differences may be, this is a universal BlindSpot that needs everyone's attention.

My Auntie Pat's story:

Auntie Pat visited us in El Paso from the east coast every few years. It was always an adventure because she was the family character. Although she was born in St. Louis, she cultivated a slight British accent and threw British phrases around all the time. She also behaved with great flare and drama, sometimes amusing my family and sometimes causing big scenes that weren't amusing in any way.

The last time she visited, we'd taken her across the border to Juarez, Mexico and drilled her on the procedure for coming back to the US side. We'd had a number of friends who decided to be "cute" with the Mexican border guards and their actions resulted in some serious consequences. We told Auntie to just say "American" when the border guard asked for citizenship and leave it at that.

When Auntie reached the border guard and he asked, "What are you?" to our horror she sighed and said, "Just tired." There was the expected reaction from the Federales and it took a lot of polite apologizing to get Auntie back to the states. It goes without saying that we never quite relaxed whenever we took her to Mexico.

On one trip she'd been very well behaved, so we thought we were home free. We were in a large market and all of us had gone our own way to look at what interested us. I heard Auntie's voice across the hall demanding, "Where is the loo?" I turned around and could see Auntie, hands on hips, standing with the proprietor repeating, slower and louder, "W-h-e-r-e i-s t-h-e l-o-o?" Auntie Pat stretched out each word for emphasis. The man looked concerned, glanced around for someone else to help, and said something in Spanish. Auntie Pat raised her voice and practically shouted, even more slowly and much closer to the man's nose.

"W-h-e-r-e i-s t-h-e l-o-o?" The man was looking quite distressed. He had reason to be so. Auntie was most imposing and clearly agitated.

Another tourist witnessed the scene and stopped. She asked the man, "Donde esta el bano?" The man broke into a big grin, turned to Auntie Pat, and said, "El bano esta atras."

Now Auntie looked blank. The man stepped closer and repeated more slowly and carefully, "E-l b-a-n-o e-s-t-a a-t-r-a-s." Seeing that Auntie still didn't understand, the man shouted and pointed, stretching out his words even more, "A-t-r-a-s, a-t-r-a-s!"

The tourist turned to Auntie and said calmly, "The bathroom is over there."

"Well, he should have just said so," my aunt muttered as she stomped off to the loo.

The yelling and exaggerated pronunciation didn't work in either direction. Saying the same thing, only slower and louder, did not help Auntie Pat understand Spanish nor the man understand English. It didn't help any more than doing the same thing the same way over and over helps someone who didn't get it in the first place finally get it in the second, third, or fourth place.

Winchell's story:

Valerie called her computer tech support number one day because she was having trouble with her computer. "Hi, I'm Winchell, may I have the serial number of the computer you're calling about?" chirped a pleasant voice on the phone.

Valerie and Winchell went through the ritual of identification and explanation of the problem. Finally Winchell said, "Here's what you do." He then proceeded to say a bunch of technical things that sounded like complete gibberish to Valerie.

"Winchell," she said calmly, "back up. I don't understand a word you're saying. Could you make it more simple?"

"I am making it as simple as possible," said Winchell, sounding a little miffed. And then he said exactly the same thing again.

"Well, it isn't clear to me at all," said Valerie, still hearing only gibberish.

"I am being crystal clear, miss," said Winchell, now fully annoyed.

"Well," said Valerie, getting a little annoyed herself, "I'm not getting what you're saying. It is not clear to me. It doesn't even make sense to me. Please try to say it another way."

"Miss," said Winchell in a measured fashion some people use when annoyed with children, "I am as clear as it is possible to be. I am crystal clear."

"I'll just call back later," said a defeated Valerie, who'd been there before.

Winchell obviously evaluates his clarity from his perspective – his MeFocus. He is at a BS-Xing featuring Intention-Impact issues. Notice, regardless of how many ways Valerie communicates that she is not understanding what is being said, Winchell appears to believe he is saying it properly, correctly, clearly – whether he is understandable to Valerie or not. (We're pretty sure Winchell thinks Valerie is an idiot – righteous BS.) Déjà vu . . . *where is the* loo?

When you are not being heard, regardless of how clear you think you are, there is great merit in practicing some flexibility and creativity. After all, successful communication is the goal – isn't it?

Randy's story:

> Randy and his son were standing on Main Street at Disneyland watching the parade. An Asian man and his son stood by them. At one point the Asian man turned to Randy and said something in Chinese. Randy didn't have a clue, so he explained in English that he didn't understand. Now they both were clueless.
>
> The Asian man smiled, pointed to Randy's son, who was eating an ice cream cone, held something imaginary in his hand while he pretended to lick it, and then shrugged his shoulders.
>
> Randy, understanding immediately, moved his fingers in the air like fingers walking and then pointed down the street and waved to the left.
>
> The Asian man gave Randy a "thumb's up" and Randy returned it as he watched the man and his son walk off toward the ice cream parlor.

These two men had arrived at the BS-Xing together, quickly assessed that the way they were doing something wasn't working, and changed their behavior (language, vocabulary, expression). We're guessing that if their first option hadn't worked, they would have tried something else. They both sought clarity and did whatever it took to be understood, never assuming that their way was the only way – or even that there was only one way.

With Winchell, Valerie was at a BS-Xing herself, and she made a flexible choice like the men at Disneyland.

Winchell was stuck. He was going to insist ad naseum that he was clear. He was not about to change anything in his communication technique. In his mind he was *right* and Valerie was stupid. Valerie chose to hang up and call back.

There is great power in recognizing when you're going to an empty well for water. We've seen people trudge back and forth with an empty bucket for years before deciding to go to a different well. We've also seen people hit themselves in the head with their own empty bucket. So, "Good for Valerie." She found another way to get what she needed rather than spending any more time throwing her bucket into the sand.

When you arrive at a BS-Xing and insist on continuing to do the same thing, even when it clearly isn't working – you'll never find a loo.

It's like that old story. A person walks down a street and falls in a hole. They finally drag themselves out only to return to the same street the next day and fall in again. This time they yell at the hole. And they repeat the falling and yelling until they decide to walk around the hole. But it's a narrow street and they lose their balance and topple in once again. Finally, after being in the hole enough times and yelling themselves hoarse, they decide to go down another street.

You may have to fall in the hole a few times before you decide to try another street.

We're suggesting that as you get better and better at spotting your BlindSpots, you may not have to go in the hole more than once. You may even learn to avoid the hole in the first place.

Ben's Story:

> Ben was describing a business presentation to his associates, explaining how it all started to go awry about half-way through his talk. Ben said that as he watched the audience, they all had weird looks on their faces. And he began to notice that every time he showed a slide, most of them flinched.
>
> But Ben had lots of wonderful slides and couldn't resist sharing them. "I couldn't stop," he told his friends. There were slides, slides, and more slides, until the VP sitting in the front row interrupted Ben saying, "I think we've seen enough slides."
>
> "I knew I was in a hole and I just couldn't stop digging."

At least Ben knew he was in a hole. Many people don't. And Ben knew he was digging it deeper. People miss that too. Ben knew there was a BS-Xing, but he just couldn't put on the brakes. So, what keeps him digging? It could be his MindSet, his Spin, his perspective, or his habits. Whatever it is, he's Spotted BS at the BS-Xing. Now he has to decide what he wants to do about it.

Whether you're just starting to see the hole, are stuck in a hole, or are falling in a hole once again and screaming your brains out (literally), think of it as just another BlindSpot that's come out from behind the curtain.

CHAPTER TWENTY-FIVE

Spot is Hiding Right Under Your Nose

You've seen many different kinds of BlindSpots in this book. You've learned many different approaches for Spotting and handling them. By now you know there are multiple ways to coax Spot out from behind the curtain and multiple ways to greet Spot – or Spots – when they come out. Let us remind you that a smile or a good laugh is going to be irresistible to Spot. And, best of all, you'll be able to laugh if you remember that everyone has BlindSpots.

Renda's story:

Renda was a professional speaker. She decided she wanted to create a trademark outfit consisting of black shoes, black stockings, and a black skirt – all topped with a vividly colored jacket. She wanted the outfit to look like a complete outfit, so she planned to find brightly colored jackets trimmed with black accents.

She thought it was going to be easy. For almost two years, she looked for jackets with black piping, black cuffs, black accents, black patterns – and found nothing. She spent a good deal of time and energy complaining to sales people, friends, and associates about how hard it was to find the kind of jacket she was seeking. "It can't be that hard to make a great jacket with a little bit of black on it," she would wail.

One day she found this fabulous hot pink double-breasted jacket. She put it on and stood in front of the mirror. She was ecstatic and told her friend, "Look, it's just the perfect color. And you know how I love double-breasted suits. And it's light weight. And it has black b . . ." Her voice trailed off as she looked down at the front of her jacket. Her friend asked, "Are you ok?"

"I'm ok," said Renda is a disgusted voice. "This jacket has black buttons. Black buttons! Black buttons – right here under my nose the whole time."

"So?" said her friend, fearing that she was having a breakdown right there in the store.

"Do you have any idea how many jackets I could have bought in the last two years and just changed the buttons? Black buttons," she repeated, even more disgusted. "It never crossed my mind."

Renda is like all of us. Solutions are right under our noses and BlindSpots are everywhere else.

It is so easy to get locked into a pattern. It is so easy to remain blind to your BlindSpots.

At least it used to be!
GoodSpot Hunting!

60 SecondSpot

If you're like many of us, you look for the most efficient, quickest, or easiest way to accomplish the changes you've decided to make.

Many clients have asked us, "If you could just recommend one thing for me to do to get better at finding or correcting my BlindSpots, what would it be?"

For all of you who want something short and simple, we offer the 60 SecondSpots.

Devote 60 seconds a day to a SpotSolution.

Pick one of the following and consider, contemplate, focus, notice, cogitate, percolate, meditate, facilitate, ruminate, question, investigate, wonder, illuminate, ponder, attend . . .

Set an intention to expand, to shift, to change, to grow.

Invite your whole brain to the one minute party.

Relax and play with the BlindSpots.

Admit that everyone, including you, has BS.

Laugh at your own foibles – then do something with them.

Get acquainted with your DeepIntentions.

Remember that your good Intentions are only half the story.

Ask, "How much is this behavior costing me?" – and ask it often.

Make friends with the BlindSpots – Spot, Spot, and Spot.

Make friends with your DiscomfortZone.

Notice any automatic behaviors, responses, thoughts, feelings, or reactions.

Get – and stay – curious.

Practice mental flexibility.

Find other ways – often.

Wake up to your Spins.

Make sure you are truly willing to address BlindSpots and change behaviors.

Notice your Impact on others.

Be versatile and attentive with your InclusionaryBehavior and ExclusionaryBehavior.

Recognize and acknowledge your stubbornness and righteousness.

When you're in a hole, stop digging.

Stop doing what you've always done or don't expect it to get you something different.

Learn to spot a hole even when Spot is sitting on it.

Identify the streets with the least amount of holes . . . pay attention to construction alerts . . . notice the road signs and orange barrels.

Avoid the tree branch when it's whacked you in the head.

Go back to bed if you want to, even if it's been made.

Don't leave your spouse at House Depot.

Stop delivering ice to the ice maker.

Play in your DiscomfortZone.

Face your scorpion patterns.

Move over when someone in your lane is about to run you down.

Try jumping from black to gray instead of black to white.

Lean into the downhill ski.

Be CounterIntuitive.

Use reflections to enhance your own self-awareness.

Know your MindSets.

Give yourself a BlindSpotting grade periodically.

Shift your perspective.

Remember that your perspective is just your perspective, not *the* perspective.

Consider feedback.

Dump the brown belt.

Notice when you're stuck in a pattern – any pattern.

Be patient – with yourself and others.

Look under/around/on top of/and through your BlindSpots.

Don't order the Gonzo special. No one cares!

ConnectTheDots more often.

Practice compassion, even when it doesn't make sense.

Watch out for the Begonias.

Practice good listening.

Stop, look, and listen at the BS X-ings.

Know lots of dances.

Know lots of languages.

Call someone who cares.

Find a well with water.

Get some black buttons.

Re-read this book now and then.

You'll find that all the information you've just read may seem different down the road. As you get better at one phase of BlindSpotting, other phases will make more sense.

As you practice all your new awareness, the stories will gain deeper meaning.

As your Spin changes and your MindSets become more constructive, you'll be able to Connect many different Dots.

All of the BlindSpots will then rush from under the covers, pop out from behind the curtains, venture into your awareness from wherever they have been hiding – because they are laughingly invited by you.

Then the coyotes won't be the only ones having a party.

BLINDSPOTS GLOSSARY

3Dimensional™: Concept demonstrating that psychological issues, conditions, or positions are not one dimensional. They are, especially in the case of BlindSpots, nonlinear and can produce costs, effects, and implications in multiple directions.

60SecondSpots: Short and simple suggestions which will yield results with just sixty seconds of attention every day.

AutoPilot: Automatic patterns which occur unconsciously as a result of an Intention – often completely out of your awareness.

BlindSpots: Invisible, automatic patterns of behavior, thoughts, or feelings that can sabotage your success and happiness. They are things you cannot see which are in your way. A BlindSpot can be a hidden Psychological SpeedBump.

BlindSpotted: Someone with BlindSpots. More Spots – more Spotted.

BlindSpotter: Someone who can see or who wants to see BlindSpots.

BS: An abbreviation for BlindSpots.

BS-Xing: A BlindSpot Crossing is an intersection of choices. If a BlindSpot takes precedence, you may walk into a hole.

BSQ: Your level of BlindSpotting willingness or ability. IQ for BlindSpots.

ChoicePoint: One of many Spots along the way where you have a choice to do or think something different which can change the flavor and outcome of an event or experience.

CompassionPatterns: Your abilities to show empathy or understanding, even when someone's behavior or reaction doesn't make sense.

ConnectTheDots: A process of filling in the blanks in what you notice so that things which are invisibly connected become visible.

Cost: The negative result of your choice(s) to you or others.

CounterIntuitive: Any new consideration which is different from the way you normally, habitually, or automatically think or behave.

CrushWords™: Two or more words which have been crushed together to suggest a more related or joined concept.

DeepImpact: How something affects you at a deep or core level. It is often so far under your own awareness that you don't identify it immediately.

DeepIntentions: Your most core motivation, usually attached to one or more than one of your most treasured values.

DiscomfortZone: Any place outside of your normal, habitual, comfortable zone of behaviors.

ExclusionaryBehavior: Any behavior of yours which puts another person off or rejects them from connection with you.

Fact&Fiction™: Fact is observable, verifiable, and usually agreed upon by everyone. Fiction is an interpretation of observed Facts and is subject to much disagreement.

GoodSpot Hunting: As in "Good Will Hunting . . ." (the movie).

InclusionaryBehavior: Any behavior of yours which pulls another person in or connects them to you in some way.

Intention-Impact: The two parts of an individual's experience in any interaction. Intention refers to what is meant to have occurred. Impact refers to what is actually experienced.

Intentions: Conscious and unconscious motivations for your actions.

MeFocus: Not to be confused with paying attention to yourself, MeFocus refers to a persistently egocentric perspective.

MindReading: Acting as if you truly know what another person is thinking or feeling without being explicitly told by that person.

MindSet: A composite of your perspectives and beliefs which acts as a blueprint for categories of your behavior.

PolarJump: An illogical leap to an extreme position within a polar continuum reflecting black and white thinking.

PsychoBiological: The merging of your thoughts and beliefs with your actions and reactions.

SpeedBumps: The psychological accumulation of BlindSpots which are in your path, tripping you up, slowing you down, and throwing you off.

Spin: Spin is Fiction. It is the story or interpretation you make up from Facts you experience.

SpunFact™: An observation to which Spin has already been applied on AutoPilot. You still believe it to be Fact and are unaware of your Spin.

SpotCheck: An ongoing shift in your perspective which allows you to expand the way you have seen things in the past.

SpotDoctor: Professionals, like us, who bring

observational skills and expertise to bear on BlindSpots.

SpotDoctorsRx: Prescriptions from the SpotDoctors to assist you in your BS quest.

Spot-Savvy: Your cleverness about Spot spotting.

SpotSolution: Any strategy or assignment facilitating changes in your behavior, thinking or perspective which moves you closer to seeing or unmasking a BlindSpot.

SurfaceImpact: The Impact you think a situation is having on you. What is truly provoking your reactions and feelings is often much deeper and will require some digging.

SurfaceIntentions: The reasons you think you select some behavior. SurfaceIntentions may be true, as far as they go, but there is usually something deeper, something more linked to core or survival issues too.

WoofWoof: The sound that some or all of the Spots make when there is a dot to be connected or a clue to be uncovered.